David Greig
Plays: 1
Europe, The Architect,
The cosmonaut's last message to the woman he once loved in the former Soviet Union

Europe: 'A fierce, compassionate, mighty ambitious drama.'
Scotsman

The Architect: 'The whole play vibrates with such ambition and intelligence – and in some places with such a breathtaking quality of emotional courage and openness . . . David Greig is probably the most gifted of the new Scottish playwrights of the Nineties.' *Scotland on Sunday*

The cosmonaut's last message: 'It's a play that constantly mixes the intimate and the epic, and it gets right under your skin.'
Daily Telegraph

David Greig was born in Edinburgh and now lives in Fife. His work has been staged throughout Europe, the USA and Australia. In 1990, he co-founded the Scottish theatre company, Suspect Culture for which he has written eight texts including *Timeless*, *Mainstream*, and *Casanova*. His plays include *Europe* (1994); *The Architect* (1996); *The Speculator* (1999); *Danny 306 + me (4ever)* (1999); *Victoria* (2000) and *Outlying Islands* (Traverse Theatre and Royal Court 2002). Television and film work includes: *Nightlife* (BBC Scotland, 1995, winner of the BBC Double Exposure competition); *Nothing in the Whole Wide World* (United Broadcasting); and for radio, *Copper Sulphate* (BBC Radio 3, 1997) and *The Commuter* (BBC Radio 4, 2001).

DAVID GREIG

Plays: 1

Europe

The Architect

The cosmonaut's last message
to the woman he once loved
in the former Soviet Union

introduced by Dan Rebellato

Methuen Drama

METHUEN DRAMA CONTEMPORARY DRAMATISTS

3 5 7 9 10 8 6 4

This collection first published in Great Britain in 2002 by
Methuen Publishing Limited

Methuen Drama
A & C Black Publishers Ltd
36 Soho Square,
London W1D 3QY
www.methuendrama.com

Europe first published in 1995 by Methuen Drama in *Frontline Intelligence 3*
Copyright © David Greig, 1995, 2002
The Architect first published as a Methuen Fast Track Playscript in 1996
Copyright © David Greig 1996, 2002
The cosmonaut's last message to the woman he once loved in the former Soviet Union
first published by Methuen in 1999
Copyright © David Greig 1999, 2002
Introduction copyright © 2002 by Dan Rebellato

David Greig has asserted his right under the Copyright, Designs and Patents
Act, 1988, to be identified as the author of this work

A CIP catalogue record for this book is available from the British Library.

ISBN 978 0 413 77253 4

Typeset in Baskerville by MATS, Southend-on-Sea, Essex
Printed and bound in Great Britain by
CPI Cox & Wyman, Reading, Berkshire

Caution

Contents

David Greig:
A Chronology

1991   *A Savage Reminiscence* (Suspect Culture, Hen and
       Chickens, Bristol)

1992   *Stalinland* (Suspect Culture, Theatre Zoo, Edinburgh)
       And the Opera House Remained Unbuilt (Suspect Culture,
       Theatre Zoo, Edinburgh)
       The Garden (Suspect Culture, Theatre Zoo, Edinburgh)

1993   *The Time Before the Time After* aka *Consider the Dish*
       (Rough Edge Theatre Company, Edinburgh)

1994   *Stations on the Border/Petra's Explanation* (July, Suspect
       Culture, The Arches, Glasgow)
       Europe (October, Traverse, Edinburgh)

1995   *One Way Street* (Suspect Culture, Traverse, Edinburgh)

1996   *The Architect* (February, Traverse, Edinburgh)
       Petra (May, TAG Theatre company, schools tour)
       The Stronger (after Strindberg) (May, The Brewster
       Sisters, The Arches, Glasgow)
       Airport (June, Suspect Culture, Traverse, Edinburgh)
       Nightlife (August, BBC 2)
       Copper Sulphate (BBC Radio 3)

1997   *Caledonia Dreaming* (7:84, Traverse, Edinburgh)
       Timeless (Suspect Culture, Tramway, Glasgow)

1999   *Mainstream* (February, Suspect Culture, MacRobert
       Theatre, Stirling)
       *The cosmonaut's last message to the woman he once loved in the
       former Soviet Union* (April, Paines Plough tour)

Danny 306 + Me (4 Ever) (May, Birmingham Rep and
Traverse, Edinburgh)
The Speculator (June, Mercat de la Flors, Barcelona
translated into Catalan)
The Speculator (August, Traverse at the Royal Lyceum,
Edinburgh)

2000 *Outside Now* (January, Prada Showroom, Milan)
Swansong (February, BBC Radio 4)
Candide 2000 (March, Suspect Culture, Old Fruit
Market, Glasgow)
Oedipus (after Sophocles) (Tramway and Theatre Babel,
Old Fruitmarket, Glasgow)
Victoria (April, Royal Shakespeare Company, The Pit,
London)

2001 *Casanova* (February, Suspect Culture, Tron, Glasgow)
Not About Pomegranates (July, Al-Kasaba, Ramallah,
Palestine)
Dr Korczak's Example (September, TAG, schools tour)
The Commuter (November, BBC Radio 3)

2002 *San Diego* (January, a reading at the Tron Theatre,
Glasgow)
Lament (April, Suspect Culture at the Tron, Glasgow)
Outlying Islands (May, BBC Radio 3)
Battle of Will (June, reading of a translation of *Combats
de Possédés* by Laurent Gaudé, National Theatre)
Outlying Islands (July, Traverse, Edinburgh and Royal
Court, London)

Introduction

David Greig is a central figure in an extraordinary flowering
of Scottish playwrights that emerged to international acclaim
in the 1990s. Championed by the newly rebuilt Traverse
Theatre, Edinburgh, playwrights like Greig, David Harrower,
Stephen Greenhorn, and Chris Hannan created an fiery stage
poetry with which to present contemporary Scotland to the
world, mixing a powerful sense of its history with profound
care for its future.

This renaissance of Scottish playwriting coincided with a
revival of Scottish nationalism, after the dog days of the 1980s,
culminating in a vote in favour of a devolved Scottish
parliament in 1997 and the inauguration of that body two
years later. No doubt Scotland's growing cultural confidence
fostered developments in the political sphere and vice versa
though none of these playwrights could be described as
straightforwardly nationalistic in their plays. David Greig once
wrote that 'any playwright who tells you they're a nationalist is
either a bad playwright or a bad nationalist'. After the political
and military campaign for Italian unification achieved its goal
in the mid-nineteenth century, Italian statesman Massimo
D'Azeglio supposedly said, 'Italy has been made; now we must
make the Italians'. Despite a reluctance to be tied down by
Nationalist slogans the new playwrights of the 1990s have
been playing a vital role in exploring what a devolved
Scotland might mean for the Scots. None of them has played a
more vitally searching role in this than David Greig.

David's writing career began in 1990 with *Savage
Reminiscence*, a short play imagining Caliban's life after the
events of Shakespeare's *The Tempest*. This was performed by
Graham Eatough, with whom David founded Suspect
Culture, now one of Scotland's leading touring theatre
companies. As a core part of Suspect Culture's 's creative
team, which also includes composer, Nick Powell, and
designer, Ian Scott, David has written the text for several

x   David Greig Plays

shows including *Airport* (1996), *Timeless* (1997), *Mainstream* (1999), *Casanova* (2001) and *Lament* (2002). He has also worked independently as a playwright since 1994, being produced by some of the leading theatres in Britain: *Europe* (1994), *The Architect* (1996), *The Speculator* (1999) and *Outlying Islands* (2002) were produced by the Traverse Theatre, with the latter transferring to the Royal Court. *Caledonia Dreaming* (1997) was a huge success for 7:84, and *The cosmonaut's last message to the woman he once loved in the former Soviet Union* (1999) gained applause and strong critical notices during its tour with Paines Plough. *Victoria* (2000) was produced by the Royal Shakespeare Company and he has also produced a string of fine radio plays. His work has been seen all over Europe and increasingly, in America. There have been plays for children – *Petra* (1996) and *Dr Korczak's Example* (2001); a play with puppets *Danny 306 + Me (4 Ever)* (1999), a film for BBC Scotland, *Nightlife* (1996), and some adaptations from Sophocles, Jarry and Strindberg.

The consistency of David's output of work is remarkable and the strength of his writing has been quickly recognised by other writers. In November 1998, his friend and fellow playwright, Sarah Kane, admitted to me her astonishment at his ability to produce so much extraordinary and beautiful work. A year later, I was part of a residential week at the Royal Exchange Theatre, Manchester, which brought together a group of young playwrights to share and debate ideas about theatre writing, theatre making, entertainment, culture and art. Disagreements were frequent and often heated, but the one thing that we all agreed on was our admiration for the work of David Greig.

It may seem odd to describe the writer who once wrote 'I certainly hate Scotland', as providing a service to the Scottish national cause. Scattered through the plays there are barbed asides at his country's expense: in *The Speculator* Lord Islay's statement that 'the advantage of being Scottish is there's always somewhere better to go' always raised generous self-mocking laughter from its Edinburgh audience. In *Caledonia Dreaming*, Stuart McConnachie, a Member of the European Parliament, became a good-natured figure of satirical fun for his hopeless ambition to bring the Olympic Games to Edinburgh. Many of Greig's characters are even more sharply hostile to the country of their birth, from Euan's claim in *Victoria* that 'In Glasgow there's rubbish lying in the streets, strikes everywhere, folks sat on their arses all day moaning like janitors. We're a nation of bloody janitors' to Mrs Tennant's rather more terse judgment in *Casanova* that Scotland is 'cold and mean and ashamed, and repressed, and violent and . . . straight . . . This is a country which badly needs a fuck'.

I'd suggest that David sees little merit in simplistic and narrow definitions of Scottish national identity because it's the very slipperiness of Scottishness that is its prime virtue. In *Caledonia Dreaming*, Stuart's attempt to find a figurehead to stand for everything that is modern Scotland founders on the unbridgeable contradictions he finds there:

> Scotland is modern, yet old.
> Urban, yet rural.
> Friendly, yet canny.
> Strong, yet compassionate.
> Who is it?
> Who's Scotland? That's the question we need to answer.

In *The Architect*, something of the same confusion affects the lorry driver, Joe, when he's asked what Glasgow is like. Initially, he calls it friendly, but when asked about its violent reputation, uneasily settles on 'violent but friendly. That's supposed to be the characteristic'.

This ambiguity, this coexistence of irreconcilables that makes up modern Scotland is undoubtedly connected with its double status: its proud sense of nationhood and cultural separateness as opposed to its position as only one area of a small archipelago off the coast of Europe. Scotland is both itself and not quite itself; there are rich and vivid alternative maps to be drawn of Scotland's imaginary geography, depicting the thick concentrations of historical memory and the flowing urban landscapes of cultural internationalism. I think David has identified a genuine value in Scotland's mercurial identity and his plays seek to insist on it, exploit and

intensify it, refusing the simplistic blandishments of
'Braveheart' nationalism.

Whether they are set in and around Edinburgh, like *The
Architect*, in an unnamed central European country, like *Europe*,
or whether they find themselves leaving the earth altogether as
in *The Cosmonaut*, David's plays are always about Scotland. But
it is *because* they are about Scotland that they are about
everywhere. Scotland's double character, a nation in itself and
also an adjunct to various larger national and supranational
entities (England, Europe, The West, The North), gives it a
particular perspective on the world. It would be a mistake, as
David has argued, to see small countries like Scotland as
striving to imitate their bigger neighbours: 'In fact they're
quite different. A little guy's outlook is different from a big
man's'. Scotland's marginality gives it a critical, as well as
geographical, distance from the centres of global power, and a
position from which to criticise the world.

One very striking thing about David's work, something that
sets him apart from the majority of his contemporaries, is the
conscious and artful way in which he is trying to come to
terms with the immense changes being wrought across the
world by globalisation: a perspective shaped and enhanced by
his experience of a multiple and ambiguous Scotland. Over
the last thirty years, under the direct and indirect influence of
the World Bank, World Trade Organisation, the International
Monetary Fund and with the complicity of most of its
governments, the Northern hemisphere has seen an awesome
acceleration in the construction of a global free market. Trade
barriers, exchange controls, all restrictions on the movement
of goods, money and services across national boundaries are
being eroded or swept away. As a result, those national
boundaries are becoming more and more permeable, and less
and less meaningful.

But Scotland has had a permeable border for hundreds of
years and knows well the precariousness of belonging to a
culture shaped from beyond its border by the pitiless forces of
trade and finance. In the first half of the nineteenth century,
absentee landlords wishing to extract greater profit from their
Highland estates ruthlessly forced the tenant farmers from

their crofts, burning their cottages, evicting their families, often to make way for enormous and more profitable sheep farms. These farms would be tended and managed by farmers from the Lowlands and across the border in England. In many ways this was an early act of 'globalisation', as the entrenched territorial traditions were swept away by the international flows of capital. Now, of course, the scale and power of global capital is even greater. In *Victoria*, a play which spans three generations in the West Highlands, a mountain whose very rock in the 1930s seemed to hold on to its inhabitants, thwarting their attempts to escape, has, by the end the nineties, been levelled, ground down to make aggregate by a mining corporation. This corporation's name is 'Sutherland Granite Aggregates', which recalls the Sutherland estate that in the 1810s saw some of the most barbaric episodes in the history of the Highland clearances.

The imprint of globalisation is unusually deep in David's work. Globalisation is often described not only as a form of economic expansion but an expansion of consciousness. We feel ourselves to be citizens of the world. The conduit for this sensibility is, of course, the expansion and acceleration of our global transport and communication networks. A cultural by-product of this is what French anthropologist Marc Augé has called 'non-places': a proliferation of temporary transit and service points designed to facilitate our accelerated access to other places. Think of airport terminals, internet cafés, motorway service stations, shopping malls. These are passing places, severed from history, functional, offering strictly temporary satisfactions – the seats in some fast-food restaurants are deliberately designed to become quickly uncomfortable ensuring maximum 'customer throughput'.

These are characteristically the places in which David's plays are set: from *Europe*'s waiting rooms and coach stations to *The Cosmonaut*'s airports, hotels, and bars, passing through *The Architect*'s bleak nights on the motorway network. This severance from history is particularly important to Scotland where national identity is often linked with the defence of cultural memory. Yet Scotland's major urban centres have been reshaped under the rationalising force of technological modernisation, impelled on and on by the demands of global capital. In *The Architect*, Sheena Mackie describes the transformation of the Docklands by the arrival of 'containerisation' in the 1970s, where imported goods could be loaded straight from ship to lorry, which obviated the need for docks in major towns. Huge areas of major cities – London, Manchester, Liverpool, Bristol, as well as Glasgow and Edinburgh – that were once given over to loading and unloading, shipping and distribution, were laid waste and then redeveloped as leisure complexes, offering bars, night clubs, museums, restaurants and shopping facilities. It appears to be in one such bar that Suspect Culture's *Timeless* is set.

These leisure complexes often feature romanticised museums offering an opportunity to experience the sights, sounds and smells of the former dockyards and shipyards on which they were built. And just as the city begins to understand itself through its simulacra, so perhaps, a certain alienation creeps through Scottish consciousness. In *The Architect*, all the characters seem only to understand themselves through their images and ideals. Despite the evident wreckage of a family around him, Leo Black announces at the dinner table, 'We should eat together more. As a family . . . Everyone round the table. Do the washing up together'. Billy kisses Martin when he sees their image together in a shop window. When Paulina announces that she wants Leo to leave the family home, she remarks that he won't really miss her: 'When you leave you'll notice a wife-shaped space'. Dorothy gets picked up hitch-hiking on the motorway and goes with the driver into the container on the back of his lorry. The sexual encounter misfires as it becomes clear she has lost any sense of what she actually wants, seeking only some affirmation in the desires of another: 'You have to say. You have to tell me. How do you want me to be? How Joe?'

The economic transformations of the last twenty years have seen Scotland's industrial profile shift from shipbuilding, mining, steel, and agriculture to the tertiary industries of tourism, information technology, services and com- munications. In some respects this has left rural Scotland

behind; certainly many Scots have left the countryside, and
the flight to the cities has intensified over this period. There
has long been a tension between urban and rural Scotland,
but as the city closes itself in within its simulacra, its familiarity
with the country recedes ever further into the haze of cultural
forgetting. In *The Architect*, city-bound Martin feels the need to
rediscover some space of Edenic purity in which he can refind
himself through. He believes the country might hold just such
a place – 'Some wilderness. Somewhere with mountains' – but
his plan to find an old deaf man in the mountains who can
teach him how to turn wood and make tables, he reveals only
the imaginative barriers between the country and the city.

David's plays certainly do not pine for a pre-lapserian 'true'
Scotland; if anything they are more at home in the neon-lit
theme bars of modern Glasgow than in the glens and braes of
the West Highlands. And perhaps it is false to compare
authentic traditional Scotland with its globally-traversed
descendent. It can be hard to say what authentic Scotland
really means. In *Airport*, a Scottish traveller identifies his
nationality to a Spanish check-in clerk with a few short cut
emblems of his nationality: malt whisky, the Loch Ness
Monster and kilts (and he unwisely attempts a Highland Fling
to emphasise this point). Malt whisky I think we can leave
alone, but the other two sound a slightly ironic note: the Loch
Ness Monster is at best legendary, and the tartans of all the
Scottish clans may be no less so. Far from being the ancestral
clan uniform of the Scots as they are sometimes made to
appear, the array of tartans carefully labelled and
distinguished in every Highland tourist shop were to a very
large extent invented in 1822, when George IV paid a royal
visit to Edinburgh:

> The king spent two weeks in the Scottish capital and a
> series of extraordinary pageants, all with a Celtic and
> Highland flavour, were stage-managed by Sir Walter
> Scott for his delectation. What ensued was a 'plaided
> panorama' based on fake Highland regalia and the
> mythical customs and traditions of the clans.[1]

Scottishness, like Nessie and the Great Haggis Hunt, has perhaps always been, to some extent, an invention designed for cross-border consumption.

The plays gathered here show the theatrical development of David's attempt to confront the meanings of nationhood, identity, globalisation and freedom. *Europe*'s most immediate source was the genocide unfolding in the former Yugoslavia, but it examines the meanings of that conflict through a characteristically ambiguous set of images. The play is set in and around an obsolete railway station in a border town on the edge of a middle-European state. No more compelling image could be offered of the obliteration of national boundaries by the forces of globalisation than the express trains that scream past these platforms. The train is an ambivalent image, loaded with contrary historical associations. Many of them are very positive – progress, communication between peoples, the broadening effects of travel, the power of human technological endeavour – but in Fret's unconsciously fascistic imagery praising 'steel and tracks and trains like blood muscle and arteries holding the continent together', we are subliminally reminded of the infamous apologia for Mussolini, that at least he made the trains run on time.

The geographical boundaries of a country are often the arbitrary sediment of centuries of historical processes. Yet they can take on symbolic importance in the national imagination and any penetration of these boundaries, real or imagined, can cause a convulsion of national feeling. In *Europe*, with borders and territorial divisions in flux, national sentiment is shown in its darkest forms. The wolves that hunt the forests around the station, coming out at night to make raids on the town, suggest the gathering threat of fascism that is not expunged by globalisation but perhaps provoked by it. The links are shown in the person of Morocco, a successful entrepreneur who returns home to hymn the magic of international finance; for him a border is 'a magic money line. See. You pass something across it and it's suddenly worth more. Pass it across again and now it's cheaper. More . . . less . . . less . . . more . . . . fags, drink, jobs, cars . . . less is more, more or less . . . see . . . magic money just for crossing a magic line'. The same magic, and the same principle of accumulation, would also be the subjects of Greig's *The Speculator*, about the eighteenth-century Scots banker, John Law, whose scheme for issuing bank notes in place of gold and silver was the beginning of today's dematerialised global network of virtual financial transactions.

Yet the more weightless the flows of capital, the more threatened and compromised the sense of identity, and the more vigorous become attempts to reassert it by excluding imagined others. The points at which they clash are moments of sexual and racial violence. In *Europe*, the intimate interconnections between the dilution of national identity and the flows of global trade are starkly realised in a series of thrilling, beautiful and brutal stage images. By the end of the play, as a group of unemployed furnacemen burn down the station killing Fret, Adele and Katia thunder out of town on an express train murmuring the names of European cities, while the arsonist recalls how news of the stationmaster's murder spread across Europe. The image is of a sudden lifting, a pulling of focus that moves outward from the town, drawing in the names of those cities, redrawing the map of Europe in the heat and light of that murderous conflagration.

The view from above is a common motif in David's work. It is connected in some ways with his interest in seeing the larger international context, but more often than not it is associated with aloofness, isolation, distance, a fear of others. In *The Architect*, Sheena Mackie is a resident of Eden Close, the housing estate designed by Leo Black, the play's eponymous architect. She is determined to get his support to have the flats demolished and he is equally determined to persuade her that they are good flats. They stand around an architectural model, as Leo vainly explains that 'the original design was, in fact, loosely based on Stonehenge' and recalls that the plans won him an award. The arrangement of the family, standing around and looking down on these flats, is a powerful visual emblem of the coolly impersonal perspective of the architect, as Leo directs her attention to the abstract symmetry of the blocks. As Sheena remarks, 'were the judges in the helicopter when they gave you the award?'. This image of physical abstraction also underlines Leo's aloof lack of involvement in the real lives of the people living in his designs, which spills out in an embarrassing outburst: 'I'm sorry. I won't see good ideas blown up just because some people can't see beyond their own misery'.

This theme of genteel elevation is picked up elsewhere in the play. Leo's wife, Paulina, claims to rather fancy the idea of living in a high rise: 'Height's a strong point. You don't want to be in amongst it. Ground floors attract opportunist thieves. I don't imagine they bother with the tenth. On the tenth you can watch it all happening down below. Rise above it all'. This desire to float effortlessly above human society seems to underlie her shuddery advice to Martin to change his jacket unless he wants to attract other people: 'Even if you don't actually talk to them. They come into your proximity. You should be careful'. This advice has clearly rubbed off on her son, since Martin admits that he likes creeping onto the roofs of tall buildings where there are 'no people, no sound, no signals, no feeling'. Elsewhere his disgust with other people spills out in a revolted speech that associates communication with bodily waste and contamination: 'When people talk they clog your head with shit. The shit they talk gets in your head and slops around. More and more shit'.

This ambivalence is very pertinent to globalisation. On one level, the rise in communication and travel has numerous advantages, and a global consciousness might put a stop to some of the worst effects of global capitalism. On the other, sheer faith in the 'invisible hand' of the global market in righting all wrongs can seem fetishistic and impersonal. In 1999, James Wolfensohn, the president of the World Bank, describing the system of global finance admitted, 'at the level of people, the system isn't working'. This is a curiously Leo-like remark – if it's not working at the level of people, at what level *is* it working? In Suspect Culture's 2002 show, *Lament*, the tendency for the global economic perspective to rise irresponsibly beyond sight of people on the ground was painfully evoked:

And the bankers, the politicians
I think they must think
I don't know what they think.
The people who say – It's good for them to have fiscal discipline
I think to say that – you must be
You can't possibly believe that.
You can't possibly look at another person's life in that way.

One of the many joys of *The Architect*, though, is its
complexity. Despite the snootiness and misanthropy of
the Black family, the play does not unequivocally condemn
Leo. A profound melancholy haunts this play's vision of
contemporary Britain. Dorothy's nocturnal adventures on
the motorways afford her a metaphorical image of society;
the great stretches of motorway separating the towns may
image the chasms of suspicion and contempt that divide the
Blacks, who are themselves perhaps emblematic of the
atomised, market-driven collection of post-industrial
Britain. It is in part this melancholy that persists in
affirming something in Leo's desire for purity of design.
Leo's grand vision is clearly a vision of social, even socialist,
planning. The fortunes of such ideals have crumbled with
the fabric of Eden Court, the name of which suggests a
paradise lost, and the play does not greet its loss with any
pleasure.
    More than that the play contains subtle affirmations of the
persisting value of a view of ourselves, which is perhaps
inevitably an ariel view, as members of a society, a
community. Despite themselves, the family continually try to
make contacts, even if they are fleeting – like Martin's
anonymous sexual encounters, or Dorothy's truck drivers.
These moments might not mean too much on their own, but
they are reinforced by an enormously complex web of
echoes, parallels and shadowy after-images that seem to
overflow the strict bounds of the narrative and suggest forms
of attraction and connection not exhausted by the cynical
individualism of the everyday. The four members of the
Black family seem to be shadowed in the play by the
outsiders, Joe, Sheena and Billy. Although it is never

confirmed, tiny hints – a shared liking for country music, Billy and Sheena's son's inclination to hurl themselves from tall buildings – allow for the possibility that they too are a family. (Billy may even be a kind of heavenly creature.) He twice tells Martin 'I can make you good' and seems convinced that he can fly. This thesis receives subtle support during the pub quiz, one answer in which is the film *It's a Wonderful Life* which is about an angel visiting the earth to save a man's soul.

Such hints and echoes affirm our interconnectedness with one another. In the truck stop, the Country-music-loving Joe half-jokingly imagines she is receiving signals from somewhere, like dolphins across the ocean floor. As he awkwardly coos his dolphin sounds, we cut to Billy and Martin on the roof, and Billy picking up Country music on his portable radio. Later in the play, Joe is alone in the cab of his lorry, listening to Emmylou Harris's 'Boulder to Birmingham'. This song, written by Harris after the death of her partner Gram Parsons, is a love song to a dead man, an impossible act of communication which is reiterated when we watch him repeat his dolphin call, signalling out to Dorothy across the spaces. The play dares us to imagine that such an act is possible, a kind of alternative globalisation, a utopian reduction of the physical spaces between people in an act of hopeless beauty.

The Cosmonaut contains such a range of characters, narratives and locations that one might expect it to seem like a jumble of fragments, a postmodern pick'n'mix from the Baudrillardian hypermarket. In fact it is nothing of the kind, and the whole is pulled together by a web of connections that transcend the logic of the plot. There are moments of impossible attempts at communication – a woman in a London street shouting at an aeroplane, an astronomer randomly beaming music into space, and the climactic moment that gives the play its title: Oleg, a stranded Cosmonaut, detonates his capsule, hoping that it might be seen by a woman with whom he spent one idyllic weekend and never saw again. And the echoes can be tiny – a pack of

playing cards, a way of describing Bob Dylan, a momentary
groping for words, the mystery of 'stuff'. Throughout the
play, Vivienne is seeking her runaway husband, Keith, but
the same actor also plays Sylvia, whose husband also left her.
At the very end of the play, the text informs us that Sylvia
walks into the bar and sees Keith. On stage, of course, it is
hard entirely to know which woman has found Keith, or even
who she's found. These ghostly doublings, these corporeal
puns, emphasise, beyond the power of the narrative, the
connections between people that exceed the social wedges
that consumerism has driven between us.

Doublings are at the heart of David Greig's work, which
insists on a global perspective as well as local engagement,
sees what divides us as well as what connects us. Greig's
work is always at least two things at once, much like
Scotland. Always being one thing and something else,
Scotland provides, in some ways, the model for David's
theatre. What all of these imaginative devices do is unsettle
the stranglehold of what *is* on what *might be*, reaching out
beyond the actual *to something else*. In the Suspect Culture
show *Candide 2000*, which relocates Voltaire's novel to
Clearwater, a contemporary shopping mall, a chorus of
truant mallrats intone its numbed globalised virtues: 'You
can eat Chinese food / Indian food / Mexican food / Italian
food / French food / American food / All different countries
/ That's what it's like'. Rather like the injunctions to 'get
real' or 'face facts', 'that's what it's like' extinguishes any
thought of what *might be* by dumbly insisting only on what *is*.
David's plays, and his work with Suspect Culture, break with
the highly populist Scottish theatre traditions of Borderline,
Wildcat, or 7:84. As a result there is perhaps still an idea
around that these works are somehow less political than
those they succeeded.

In fact, this is the political theatre for a globalising world.
David once wrote that 'political theatre has at its very heart
the possibility of change', and as resistance seems ever more
useless in the face of impossibly powerful corporations
operating with the complicity of our supine governments,
preserving this possibility is ever more urgent. Perhaps it is in

fact in the beauty of David's writing that we can continue to
remind ourselves that there is value beyond calculation,
beyond economic value. His doublings, ghostings, paradoxes
and parallels, serve to open up the world around, to insist that
whatever it may be like, there is also the possibility of
something else.

By insisting on this paradoxical doubled and undefinable
Scotland, David Greig's work is trying to preserve a radical
space in the simplifications of a politics based on national
identity. This is where nationalism can benefit from the
playwright; it is also where England and the other *soi-disant*
'major powers' can learn from Scotland. Because in David's
work, despite the self-deprecating talk of Scotland's dour,
crabit reputation, there is a tremendous affirmation, an
evocation of a better world, even a sense of utopia. In
Caledonia Dreaming, Stuart McConnachie's dreams of an
Edinburgh Olympics are in many ways risibly impractical.
And yet there is something heart-swellingly fine in the
moment where he describes the opening ceremony,
something that transcends the absurdity of the aspiration and
affirms aspiration itself, in a way that reaches out to the
utopian in all of us:

> A massed pipe band play 'Flower of Scotland'
> And the stadium roof starts to move!
> A chink of evening sunshine splits the stadium in half
> The light getting brighter as the roof retracts.
> The crowd are dazzled.
> The Olympic flame is lit.
> And suddenly . . .
> There are a thousand Highland dancers.
> And a thousand bagpipers.
> And down from the sky come flowers . . .
> Hundreds of thousands of flowers . . .
> The Flowers of Scotland!
> Each one representing the people who're coming home.
> From the Clearances, Culloden, the war, all the people
> who've went to London or America or Newfoundland . . .
> D'you see . . .

The flower of Scotland is coming home.
And over the tannoy we hear . . .
Spoken in a deep rich voice . . .
'For a' that and a' that
A man's a man for a' that'

Dan Rebellato
Royal Holloway, June 2002

Notes

1 The Scottish Nation 1700–2000, T. M Devine (Penguin,
2000; p.235)

Europe

To Graham, Alan, Harriet and Phil

But where shall we go to today, my dear?
But where shall we go to today?

Auden, 'Refugee Blues'

Something unique is afoot in Europe, in what
is still called 'Europe' even if we no longer
know very well what or who goes by this name.

Derrida, *The Other Heading*

Europe was first performed at the Traverse Theatre, Edinburgh, on 21 October 1994. The cast was as follows:

Morocco	David Baker
Fret	Alasdair McCrone
Berlin	John Kazek
Adele	Louise Ironside
Katia	Sharon Maharaj
Sava	Finlay Welsh
Horse	Gregory Haiste
Billy	Michael Nardone

Chorus   Played by members of the company

Directed by Philip Howard
Designed by Kenny MacLellan
Lighting by Michael Calf
Music by John Irvine

Characters

Morocco, *a local entrepreneur*
Fret, *the stationmaster*
Berlin, *a worker*
Adele, *the porter*
Katia, *a foreigner*
Sava, *a foreigner*
Horse, *a worker*
Billy, *a shop steward*

Setting: A small decaying provincial town in Europe. Autumn.

Act One

1 Morocco

Darkness . . .

An international express train passes the station. The train makes an incredible noise, building steadily as it approaches. Speed, metal and light dominate the theatre drowning everything for a moment in the train's elemental force. Slowly, as the sound dies, the lights come up.

Morocco *arrives in the town square. He is a dark man, unshaven and wearing a dusty suit and sunglasses. He has a heavy suitcase with him. In front of a blue neon sign for the calypso BAR he lights a cigarette, puts his suitcase down and considers his situation.*

2 The First Chorus

1 Ours is a small town on the border, at various times on this side,

2 and,

3 at various times,

2 on the other,

1 but always

1,2,3 on the border.

4 We're famous for our soup,

5 for our factory which makes lightbulbs

1 and for being on the border.

6 On the plains at the heart of Europe

7 we're checkers of passports and clippers of tickets,

8 manufacturers of soup and light.

6   Europe

1   History has washed across us

2   in armies driving first west

3   then east

2   then west again.

4   Wave upon wave has crashed about us,

All   but we've remained,

5   a rockpool on the shoreline,

6   inhabitants of the tidemark,

7   the place where driftwood is deposited,

8   beyond the cleansing reach of the waves.

1   Some places become used to the thud of industry.

2   Some places become used to the music of a cafe piano.

3   But here, in the interior,

4   we've become used to the stillness,

5   to the rhythm of the railway timetable

6   and the rustle of currency.

All   We ask for very little here.

7   With things as they are we daren't ask for much.

8   Except that as you pass,

5   on your way to an older,

6   more beautiful

7   or more important place,

8   you remember that we are,

All   in our own way,

1   also Europe.

Express train passing.

3 Arrivals

*The town's station on an autumn morning. The station's architecture
bears witness to the past century's methods of government. Hapsburg,
Nazi and Stalinist forms have created a hybrid which has neither the
romantic dusting of history, nor the gloss of modernity. The predominant
mood is of a forgotten place. Timetables, out-of-date posters and sadly
decrepit information signs hang from the walls. A plain wooden bench sits
in the middle of the main hall. The floor is of dirty concrete and is
unswept.*

Fret *is in his office. We can't see him.*

*In the corner of the waiting room is a blackboard with the chalked sign
'NO TRAINS' written in bold letters.*

Adele *is on the station roof watching trains. A bundle of notebooks and
brochures are arranged beside her. She hasn't seen* **Berlin** *arrive behind
her.*

Sava, *a man in his late fifties, is sitting on the station bench, asleep
huddled pathetically amongst belongings: a canvas bag, some
polythene bags and an old suitcase. His clothes have not been changed
for some weeks, perhaps months. They were not fashionable clothes to
start with.*

Katia, *his daughter, sits next to him, straight-backed, awake.*

Fret   ADELE! ADELE, WHERE ARE YOU?

The train's noise subsides.

Fret (*emerging from the office carrying a bundle of timetables*)   Adele,
I can't make head nor tail of these can you come and have a
look please. (*Noticing* **Katia** *and* **Sava**.) Oh.

Berlin   Adele.

Fret   Are you?

Adele   It's you. (*Checking her watch.*) Ten past nine.
(*She ticks it off in her notebook.*) Shouldn't you be at work?

Fret   You're not? You're not?

Berlin   Fret said you'd be here.

Fret   Are you?

Adele   Isn't it beautiful? Look. Before it disappears.

Berlin   Yes. Adele. I.

Fret   Obviously not.

Fret, *believing they must be there for a reason, tries to ignore their presence.*

Berlin   Adele, I . . .

Fret   I need you to have a look at these timetables.

Adele   There, follow my hand – there! Where the track curves before the bridge . . . past the checkpoint . . . there! (*She points.*)

Fret   Now! Please!

Adele   Can you see it?

Berlin   I can see it. Look, Adele, I've been . . .

Fret   You're not waiting for a train or anything, are you?

Adele   It's going to Warsaw. Imagine . . . Warsaw.

Fret   Only you do realise there aren't any.

Fret *lays the timetables on the floor and attempts to study them.*

Berlin   I . . . had a surprise today.

Fret   Trains, I mean.
None.
They're all cancelled.

Berlin   A shock, in fact. I had a shock.

Fret   For today, at least.

Adele   I've never been to Warsaw.

Fret   None stopping.

Berlin   There was an announcement in the canteen.

Adele   I've unloaded parcels from Warsaw. I've sold tickets to Warsaw. I've seen Warsaw in pictures, but I've never been.

Berlin   Over breakfast in the canteen.

Adele   Never actually.

Berlin   Billy told us two hundred jobs were going.

Fret   You realise there's no point in.

Berlin   Over breakfast, he said there wasn't enough work. 'I'm sorry about that, lads.' He said,

Fret   It pains me to say it.

Berlin   'Sorry, lads.'. . . Like he was saying there wasn't enough ham.

Fret   A station is a place for trains, after all.

Berlin   Not enough work for us all to have some. That's the bottom line. He said.

Fret   It's a fair mistake to make . . . but there is a sign. (*He points. They ignore him. He returns to his office.*)

Berlin   Something's got to give.
He said a consultant had been.
Someone from head office.

Fret   I'm sorry for any inconvenience.

Berlin   The consultant said we've been living in a dreamland. Four men employed to run the furnace.

Fret   ADELE, THIS DOESN'T MAKE ANY SENSE!

Berlin   'Four men. Dreamland! Cloudcuckooland, crazy' he said.

Fret   Of course it's all down to the changes.

Berlin   'You people can't be serious,' he said.

Fret   I'm sure you're aware of them.

Berlin   'I don't believe it,' he said.

Fret   The changes.

Berlin   He rolled his finger at the side of his head. 'Unbelievable.'

Fret   They're getting in everywhere.

Berlin   'Economic lunacy. Economic madness. Looks like someone's been telling you people bedtime stories.'

Fret   Like dirt.

Berlin   Someone's been telling me bedtime stories, Adele.

Fret   Muck.

Berlin   I've been sacked. Put out. Horse as well. All of us. Finished.

Fret   Waste of my time.

Berlin   What do you make of that?

Fret   Waste of your time. A great big waste.

Fret *goes back into his office.*

Berlin   Machines can run a furnace apparently. Apparently they don't need furnacemen.

Adele   Berlin . . .

Berlin   Apparently, I've been unnecessary for some time.

Adele   Berlin, maybe it means something.

Berlin   . . . not just unnecessary, Adele, but harmful as well.

Adele   Maybe it's fate. . . maybe it's God.

Berlin   It would be just like him.

Adele   It could be a sign.

Berlin   A sort of 'Piss off, Berlin, you're out' sign?

Adele   A green light.
A chance.
Do you remember we said before. . . when the border

opened. . . we said, 'What's to stop us?'
Do you remember? What's to stop us?
A factory, a job, a station.
That's all . . . a pissy job . . . nothing . . . worthless. Maybe it's
a chance, Berlin. A new start.

Berlin   You're not helping, Adele.

Adele   But you're free. Don't you see? You've been released.

Berlin   I didn't want to be released, Adele. I can't do
anything else. Working the furnace is my job. It's all I know.
There's nothing else. Nowhere else for me to go.

Adele   Look – see there . . . at the edge of the forest. You can
see the border. Just. There. You can make out the wire.

Berlin   You might as well admit I'm finished, Adele.

Adele   Nothing changes on either side of it, the landscape
stays the same, there's just the wire. Hardly visible. Like a
thought.

Berlin   Listen to me! Listen to what I'm telling you.

Adele   It's as if the border's hardly there, as if you could
imagine it away. What do you think? As if you could just walk
through it . . . just cross the line.

Berlin   You don't make any sense, Adele. You've no idea.
I'm fucked. You're fucked. We're Fucked. Fucking out of it.
Out of the fucking running. Fucked utterly.

. . .

I'm sorry.

Fret *emerges holding the fat pile of timetables in his hand, defeated.*

Fret   Adele!

Berlin   I said sorry.

Fret   ADELE!

See this? Four hundred pages and none of it makes sense.
Times, stations, trains. . . They've no relation to anything.

Meaningless . . . they might just as well be foreign.

Berlin   I didn't mean –

Fret   Foreign books. ADELE! I can only think, things must have – somewhere along the line . . . In head office they must – I don't know – I don't follow – I just think THINGS MUST HAVE COME TO SOMETHING IF THE STATIONMASTER CAN'T FOLLOW THE TIMETABLE.

Berlin   I'm sorry. We need a chance to talk . . .

Adele   I've got to go.

Berlin   Adele. Adele.

Adele *doesn't reply. She leaves.* **Berlin** *is left standing alone.*

Express train passing.

4   A breach of regulations

Katia *and* **Sava** *as before.* **Katia** *is sitting and* **Sava** *is asleep in her lap. During the scene* **Sava** *wakes up. They might exchange a few words in low voices but they don't say much.*

Adele *and* **Fret** *are pinning up the new timetables around the station.*

Fret *disappears in and out of the office during the scene fetching drawing pins, timetable sheets etc.*

Adele   She looks foreign.

Fret *coming out of office.*

Fret   They've been here since this morning.

Adele   You did say there were no trains?

Fret   They ignored me. Just sat. Didn't even look at me.

Adele   Maybe they're on business. Between meetings.

Fret   Vagrants.

Fret *in office.*

Adele   Perhaps they're tourists.

Fret   Here?

Adele   They might be . . . Or she could be a journalist . . . on the trail of a hot story.

Fret   Local Station In 'We waited for train but it never arrived' Drama.

Adele   You never know. Maybe . . . or maybe they're travelling incognito. On the run . . . spies, criminals, gun runners from Libya. Maybe they're supplying freedom fighters or terrorist factions in . . . England with plastic explosives and mortars . . . maybe she's wanted by Interpol . . . maybe she's responsible for hundreds of deaths in dozens of cities . . .

Fret *out of office.*

Fret   I don't care who they are they can't loiter on my platform. We're not a bloody youth hostel.

Adele   I don't see what harm they're doing.

Fret   It's my station.

Adele   I don't see why they shouldn't wait if they want to.

Fret   It's a breach of regulations.

Adele   Is it?

Fret   Probably . . . I don't know . . . I'm not sure but it can't be allowed to continue . . .

Adele   Why not?

Fret   Because . . . because . . . Look, Adele, I don't mean to lecture you –

Adele   But . . .

Fret *in office.*

Fret   If you want to run a station like this you have to learn you can't just let things ride. Not in this job. You have to take

control, get a hold of the reins early on . . . see what's
happening and respond effectively with action . . .

Adele   I think he looks ill. Maybe he's ill? Maybe he can't
move. She looks concerned.

Fret *out of office.*

Fret   When you're in the railways, Adele, you're connected
to the heart of things . . . so you have to keep a constant watch
on every little situation because there's always the possibility of
repercussions further along the line.

Adele *finally catches* **Katia**'s *eye. They exchange a look.*

Fret *in office.*

Fret   A little delay in Levski North because the driver wants
a sardine sandwich or a garlic sausage from the kiosk. Are you
listening? This is your training, Adele – maybe the driver was
at school with the kiosk man, maybe a mutual friend's getting
married so they have a gossip – it's possible – it's the sort of
situation a stationmaster comes across every day –

Adele   There's something . . . how would you describe it?
Something . . .

Fret   In that sausage, Adele, are the seeds of catastrophe
because the next thing is the Cracow express is kept waiting at
the points . . .

Adele   Sophisticated, she looks . . . she's not from here
anyway . . . not local.

Fret   Ten minutes maybe it waits . . . so it's late in Cracow
where it has to connect with the Paris train. An entire
transcontinental train kept waiting for ten, maybe by this
stage, fifteen minutes –

Adele   She doesn't look like she'd be local anywhere.

Sava *produces a stove from their luggage and a small bottle of water. He
proceeds to light the stove to heat up the water for coffee.*

Fret   So appointments aren't kept, businessmen apologise.

Adele   No fixed abode, a traveller.

Fret   Wives worry, husbands suspect, lovers are cheated of a few moments together, a gentle shudder across the skin of the nation because the driver of the Levski train wants a garlic sausage. You let things slide on the railways and there are repercussions . . . that's one of the few things in this life you can be sure of. You can't just let things ride.

In front of them the small stove of water is boiling. **Adele** *is watching.* **Fret** *comes out.*

Fret   (*Horrified.*)
They're cooking.
. . .
They're cooking.
. . .
They thought they'd just . . . have a cook.
On my platform.

THIS IS NOT A GYPSY ENCAMPMENT.

Determined, **Fret** *returns to his office. After a moment, the tannoy plays a short irritating tune.*

Tune.

Fret (*coughs*)   Attention please, ladies and gentlemen, attention please . . . this is a passenger announcement. There will be no trains today. Trains today have been cancelled. The next train for passengers at this station will not be for some time . . . a long time . . . until further notice . . . (*He coughs.*) We apologise for any inconvenience. This has been a passenger announcement on behalf of state railways. Thank you for your attention.

The tannoy plays a short irritating tune.

Fret *pops his head out of the office . . .* **Katia** *and* **Sava** *have taken no notice. Frustrated,* **Fret** *returns to the tannoy.*

Short irritating tune. **Katia** *notices the tune with annoyance.*

Adele   He's right.

Fret   The delay is due to . . . to –

Adele (*to* **Katia**)   The place is falling apart.

Fret   Restructuring . . . restructuring which is –

Adele   It's upsetting. He's upset . . . as you can see.

Fret   It's necessary – necessary restructuring is taking place
. . . for your benefit –

Adele   The system's collapsing . . .

Fret   And so there aren't any trains . . . Passengers are
therefore advised to make alternative arrangements.

Fret *pops his head out. Seeing they have taken no notice . . . he returns to
the tannoy in fury.*

Sava *is about to reply tentatively to* **Adele**'*s question when he is
drowned by –*

A short irritating tune.

Fret   Attention . . . Achtung. It's obviously stupid to wait for
a train when a train is obviously not coming. Please go now.

He comes out of his office.

All right. Show me your tickets.

Adele   Fret!

Katia   We don't have any tickets.

Fret   How do you expect to get on a train without proper
tickets?

Katia   We expect nothing.

Adele   He gets this way . . . he's a stickler –

Fret   You expect nothing?

Katia   Nothing.

Fret   I see.

Sava   We're making tea. Would you like some?

Fret   You do realise you're flying in the face of all reason?
. . .
You're not bloody inter-railers are you?

Sava   You wouldn't have a teaspoon of sugar at all?

Adele   I'll get it.

Fret   Stay there! Inter-railers – travelling about without a
bloody destination . . . expecting nothing . . . letting it happen
. . . getting on and off trains with complete disregard for the
principle of the thing.

Katia   Be careful of the stove.

Fret   Sleeping in stations . . . in stations, for God's sake.
International Casanovas and their Australian girlfriends. 'Let
it happen' they say . . . as though getting on a train was like
getting old, or getting sick or dying or something. Well it's not,
not in my station at any rate. In my station you buy a ticket,
you get on a train and you go where you say you're going to
go. Expect nothing. Bloody hell.

Sava   You'll hurt your foot. Boiling water will fall on your
foot.

Fret   Expect nothing! It's a passenger's job to expect
something, it's a civic responsibility . . . when you stop
expecting anything from people you're only a step away from
anarchism. Give me your pass, show me your pass!

Katia   We don't have any pass.

Fret   No pass. I see. Anarchists.

Katia   This is a waiting room . . . we're waiting. We don't
need a pass.

Adele   She's right.

Fret   All right, come on, party's over – this rubbish – all
finished now . . . (*He starts to pick up their belongings and stuff them
carelessly into their bags.*)

Sava   Watch the tea for goodness sake!

Adele   Fret!

The stove is knocked over. The water spills.

Sava   Oh dear.

Fret *cries out in pain, boiling water has poured on to his foot.*

Adele (*to* **Katia**)   I'm sorry.

Katia   I told you.

Fret   TYPICAL. THAT'S FUCKING TYPICAL.

Katia (*to* **Sava**) I told you this would happen.

Fret   Indicative . . . that's what you are. Indicative of the whole fucking situation.

Adele   I'll get the mop.

Fret   The whole thing! (*A cry of pain.*) The whole bloody thing's fucked.

Fret *sits down disconsolately nursing his foot. No one moves.*

Adele   Should I get a bandage?

Fret   Do whatever . . . just whatever . . . I don't care . . . let it happen . . .

Sava   Excuse me. We've come a long way –

Katia   We won't disturb you. We intend to be gone soon.

Sava   All we want is to spend a short while here in peace. We're not planning a coup. We're not bandits.

Katia   I can assure you, we dislike it here as much as you do.

Sava   I'm sorry if things are bad for you just now but things are bad where we come from as well. We've been blown around from place to place for a long time and this is where we've come to rest. For now. The fault is neither yours nor ours but belongs to the random chaotic winds of current events. I suggest you calm down and we'll have a look at your timetables if that's the problem . . . I've worked on the railways myself. I know the system. If there aren't any trains then we'll be in nobody's way.

Katia We're good at staying hidden. We're practised.

Sava Maybe we can even be of some use.

Katia Someone to blame if nothing else.

Sava *awaits some response.* **Fret** *has no response to give. Pause. Noise of train builds up. Express train passes.*

5 Flying boat people

Inside the Calypso Bar in the afternoon. The Calypso Bar is shabby and has counters and formica tables. The chairs are hard like school chairs. **Berlin**, **Billy** *and* **Horse** *are nursing beers.*

Berlin A video.

Horse A Datsun.

Billy Dirty books.

Berlin Beer.

Horse A trip to the mountains.

Berlin To the beach.

Billy To the sunny Med.

Horse To be naked on the sand.

Berlin To go brown in the heat.

Horse Like a pig on a spit.

Billy Surrounded by women.

Berlin Slaves.

Billy An endless supply of ice cold beer.

Horse A magical cock. A magical cock that can piss ice cold beer.

. . .

A change of mood.

Billy   Seriously, I might build a house, maybe . . .

Berlin   A cabin in the forest.

Horse   A bachelor pad.

Berlin   With your own hands . . .

Billy   Miles from anywhere.

Horse   Only the wolves for company.

Berlin   Hunt your own food . . .

Billy   Self reliance.

Horse   You could live . . .

Berlin   Until you died . . .

Billy   In the middle of the forest.

Horse   No one'd ever know.
. . .

A change of mood.

Berlin   When you think . . . When you think what . . . Fuck, I want to –

Horse   Give someone a doing.

Billy   A kicking.

Berlin   Some fuck.

Horse   That fucking consultant.

Billy   And the other cunts.

Berlin   All the fuckers.

Horse   Pan their cunts in.

Billy   Cunting pan them.

Berlin   Waste them, Billy. I want to waste them.

All   Fuckin waste the cunts.

. . .

Billy   Seriously but. What'll you do?

Berlin   Waste them. Like I said.

Horse   Who?

Berlin   Them, someone.

Billy   You wouldn't though, would you? Not really.

Horse   Why not?

Billy   Because it would be stupid.

Berlin   Would it?

Billy   Aye it would.

Berlin   Is that so?

Billy   It is.

Berlin   That's what you say is it?

Billy   Aye.

Berlin   Stupid?

Billy   Berlin.

Berlin   That's me. That's my name. So what?

A slight pause.

Horse   I think it could be good.

Berlin   What?

Horse   What you said.

Berlin   When?

Horse   Just then. What you were saying. I'm with you.

Berlin   Good.

Billy   Fine.

Berlin   Right.

. . .

A change of mood.

Horse   Did you ever see that video? The one where the bloke –

Berlin   The one where he goes mental?

Horse   Shoots everyone in the train.

Billy   Never seen it.

Horse   You'ld need to get a gun.

Billy   What happens to him in the end?

Horse   Blaze of bullets.

Berlin   Flesh flies.

Billy   Fantastic.

Horse   Brilliant. Work of a brilliant mind.

Berlin   Blood splatters all over the joint . . .

Horse   Classic of the genre.

Billy   Look at those pricks.

Horse   Where?

Billy   There. The wee cunts.

Horse   The skinheads.

Billy   Aye.

Horse   What about them?

Billy   Well . . . You didn't used to see that.

Berlin   They look under age.

Billy   Not here. You didn't used to get that in here.

Berlin   You ought to tell their dads.

Horse   Twats.

Billy   It's coming to something.

Berlin   Coming to something all right . . .

Horse   It's not right.

Billy   You're right.

Berlin   It's all wrong.
. . .

Horse   What would you do, Berlin, if you were . . . ?

Berlin   What?

Horse   In charge.

Billy   Of what?

Horse   You know.

Billy   President?

Horse   King.

Berlin   Dictator.

Horse   All of that.

Berlin   I'd . . . I'd sort it out.

Billy   How?

Berlin   I'd do the business.

Billy   You would have to face economical realities.

Horse   Harsh ones.

Billy   Stiff ones.

Horse   The cold winds of recession.

Billy   Too many workers not enough jobs.

Berlin   Yeah, well. I'm not, am I. I'm not president.

Horse   But if you were.

Berlin   I'd . . . fuck Jackie Kennedy . . . and Marilyn
Monroe, I'd buy expensive women for myself and my friends,
smart suit, smart car, smart life . . . smart.

Horse   I'd get rid of the blacks.

Berlin   Which ones?

Horse   All of them . . . boat people.

Billy   Boat People?

Horse   Steal our jobs.

Berlin   Boat People?

Horse   Apparently.

Billy   But . . .

Berlin   We're miles from the sea.

Horse   They fly them.

Billy   Flying boat people.

Horse   Apparently.

Berlin   Where did you learn that?

Horse   A bloke told me.

Billy   You should be over there with Go Balls and his mates.

Horse   Maybe I should.

Berlin   You'ld suit a skinhead.

Billy   You'ld really do it . . . if you were dictator?

Horse   First I'd give all the blacks' jobs back to us.

Billy   And then what?

Horse   Then I'd . . .

Billy   What?

Horse   Well, I'd . . .

Billy   What?

Horse   . . . fuck Jackie Kennedy . . .

Billy   And then?

Horse   I'd . . . Retire. Give it all up. Live in a hut in forest.
What about you?

Billy   I've decided already.

Berlin   What?

Billy   I'm leaving.

Horse   It's early.

Billy   Leaving here. Leaving town. Vamoose. Skidaddle.

Horse   But . . . Billy . . . Billy Bilbo . . .

Billy   Saddle up and ride my pony . . .

Horse   Old Bill . . .

Billy   Get out while the getting's good . . . I say.

Horse   My old mate Billington . . .

Berlin   Are you serious?

Billy   Couldn't be more so.

Horse   Bilboglio . . . mate . . . pal . . .

Berlin   Why?

Billy   Look around you, Berlin.
The place is fucked.
We live in a dirty, nothing place . . . it's fucked, mate.
On its way down. Sinking. Anyone can see that. You just need
to look around you . . .

Horse   The skins?

Billy   The town's sick, fading fast, last legs time.

Berlin   They're just wee boys, Billy.

Horse   They're just.

Billy   Wolves looking for scraps. Flies on shit. I'm getting
out.

Berlin   But this is where you live, Billy.

Billy   I don't live here, it's a weight, a stone in the stomach, it's not a place to live it's a place to die.

Horse   I like it.

Billy   You keep it.

Horse   Well, I never thought . . .

Berlin   Never saw you as the leaving type, Billy.

Billy   We should all leave. Get out . . . split up . . . look around.

Horse   But . . . what about . . . solidarity?

Berlin   We always said we'd stick together.

Billy   Losers stick together . . . crowds . . . sheep . . . that's sticking together . . . not me. No way I'm on my own. I've jumped ship. I'll try my luck with the sharks. Strike out. swim for the horizon while my head's above water.
. . .

Horse   Cabin in the woods for me. Fend for myself.

Berlin   I'm staying here. Staying put. Do what I can to keep sane. It's home, isn't it? Roots. I've got a wife.

Billy   Get out while you can, if you can.

Berlin   I can leave any time if I want to.

Billy   Bullshit, you're trapped.

Berlin   I just don't want to leave at this moment in time.

Billy   You're trapped.

Berlin   Fuck you I am.

Billy   You're stuck, under the bedclothes, can't get up and face the day in case the world's moved on in the night. Keep the curtains closed and lie still . . . stuck. That's you.

Berlin   Fuck you, Billy . . . I just want . . .

Horse   A magical cock that can piss cold beer.

Berlin   And a magical arse that can shit cash.

A change of mood.

Express train passes.

6   A quiet talk

At night. **Katia** *and* **Sava** *are amongst their shabby suitcases and bags.* **Sava** *has a blanket around his shoulders.* **Katia** *is obviously cold, she is smoking.*

Sava   Sit down. We can share the blanket.

Katia   I'm all right.

Sava   You'll freeze.

Katia   I'm all right.

Sava   What're you thinking about?

Katia   Nothing.

Sava   You're chewing your lip.

Katia   Am I?

Sava   When you were eight and used to take your mother's hand for the walk to school, you chewed your lip like that.

Katia   We shouldn't have stopped. We were safer travelling. Keeping moving.

Sava   You chewed your lip and frowned. While your mother smiled and passed the time with other mothers you stood at her knee and frowned like you disapproved.

Katia   I think we've made a mistake. That's all.

Sava   You held her hand and tried to pull her along the road. When the other children were kicking stones you were buttoned up, in smart shoes and your eyes fixed straight ahead. No deviations, no detours.

Katia   We'll end up stuck here. At least while we were

hidden we were flexible. We had the chance to move on.

Sava   Taking responsibility for everything. Making sure.

Katia   Now we're out in the open.

Sava   Sit down. Come on. Sit next to your dad. Give your old man a hug.

Katia   I'm not cold.

Sava   Of course you're cold. Come here.

Katia   It's fine, Dad. Look. I said I was fine.

Sava   What's the matter . . . I smell . . . is that the problem?

Katia   Dad.

Sava   You don't smell so great yourself . . . We've sweated away the summer in dirty camps. The bus was an oven. An overcrowded oven. We're bound to smell a bit . . . come on . . . sit. Stop worrying. We'll be all right.

Katia   I've made a plan.

Sava   Another one.

Katia   There won't be any trains here, the stationmaster said so himself. It's pointless staying. So we'll have to hitch. If you stand back from the road and I get cleaned up a bit we'll get lifts easily, if not we'll keep walking. In a bigger place we can get lost. We can find papers, passports, contacts . . . something. First we need to get out of here. Berlin maybe . . . Paris. Milan. Somewhere big, I'm not sure yet. I just know we can't stay here. It's too small. We're too visible.

Sava   I'm tired of plans, Katia.

Katia   I'll get a job in a club or a bar. We'll get a room.

Sava   You don't want to work in a club. You've been to college. You belong in an office . . . somewhere clean, somewhere modern.

Katia   A bar . . . something . . . whatever . . . then we can start. A room, some money.

Sava   A bar . . . it's so undignified.

Katia   A room and some money first and I'll worry about dignity later.

Sava   You plan too much. Tomorrow's tomorrow . . . tonight it's late, we've come a long way, try to sleep.

Katia   I've got things to work out.

Sava   You'll make yourself ill.

Katia   I'm trying to be realistic. I'm trying to assess the options. We can't stay here.

Sava   A station's as good a place as any. I like stations. They make me feel at home.

Katia   We'll get sent back, they'll leave us to rot in some transit camp over the border.

Sava   Maybe. I don't think so.

Katia   I've seen it happen.

Sava   You underestimate people.

Katia   Believe me, they invented hate in places like this. There's not much other nightlife. I've seen it before. I saw it at home.

Sava   You underestimate human nature. It's human nature to be suspicious at first. But you forget that it's also human nature to see the truth of a situation when the situation's made clear. That's what you forget. We're dignified people. We're decent people. These things are valued everywhere.

Katia   You still don't see it, do you?

Sava   I don't see it the way you do.
. . .
Katia, we're not in some savage country on the other side of the world. Look around you, look at the architecture. Listen to the sounds from the street. You can smell the forest. We're a long way from home but we're still in Europe. We'll be looked after. Our situation will be understood.

Katia   Europe. Snipers on the rooftops, mortars in the
suburbs and you said: 'This is Europe . . . we must stay in
Europe.' So we stayed, even after the food ran out: 'This is
Europe.' When the hospitals were left with nothing but
alcohol and dirty bandages. I warned you and you still said:
'This is Europe. Honesty will prevail, sense will win, this war is
an aberration . . . a tear in the fabric. In time it'll be sewn up
again and things will look as good as new.'

Sava   What are you saying?

Katia   I'm saying I believed you.

Sava   It was the truth. It still is the truth. Katia, the
important thing is that we never give in to animalism, to
barbarism.

Katia   At least animals protect their own.

Sava   So. This is what you wanted to talk about.

Katia   Maybe.

Sava   Say it then.

Katia   We stayed and . . . We stayed.

Sava   Go on.

Katia   It doesn't matter.

Sava   Say what you mean to say.

Katia   Forget it. I just think we should move on.

Sava   Is that everything?

Katia   Yes.

Sava   That's all you want to say.

Katia   For now.

Sava   Then it's late. We'll talk about it in the morning.

Katia   Sure.

Sava   Come and share the blanket.

Katia   I'm all right.

Express train passing.

7   Look what Berlin found on the steps

Inside the Calypso Bar. **Horse** *and* **Billy** *are drinking.* **Berlin** *enters with* **Morocco**. **Morocco** *is uneasy.*

Berlin   Horse, Billy, look what I found.

Horse   Morocco!

Billy   I don't believe it.

Berlin   On the steps of the hotel.

Morocco   The hotel.

Berlin   Dark suit, smart, dark glasses, really smart.

Morocco   I do what I can.

Billy   Long time no see, Morocco.

Morocco   Too long.

Berlin   What did I say when I saw you? What did I say.

Morocco   . . .

Berlin   I said . . . fuck me. I said fuck me.

Morocco   He did. He said that.

Berlin   I said it because I love this man. I love him. I've loved him since we were both so high and he used to sell me dirty pictures he'd stolen from you boys . . .

Morocco   No.

Billy   So that's where they went.

Berlin   If you can't rip off your friends, who can you rip off.

Horse   Morocco the porno dealer!

Morocco   I didn't do it . . . he's making it up for effect.

Berlin   Our local entrepreneur.

Billy   I'm surprised you came back. I thought you were gone for good.

Morocco   I missed the old place. I missed it. Honest to God I swear. I missed you boys. I missed the bar. I've been all over the continent from the Baltic to Gibraltar but even an entrepreneur has feelings . . . I missed it.

Berlin   I don't believe you. The only thing you worry about missing is the chance to buy dollars.

Morocco   I pined. I swear. That's the only word for it. Pined. Worse than any dog. Alone in the train from Vienna to Belgrade I passed the time with dreams of home . . . I knew I had to come back in the end.

Horse   What are you selling this time, Morocco?

Morocco   Selling? Nothing. Nothing . . . not today . . . today I've come with nothing except presents . . . see . . .

He opens his suitcase.

Vodka.

Horse   Jesus.

Morocco   One each . . . see . . . friends. (*He gives them each a bottle.*) Now. A toast . . . to the boys. I heard the bad news. The factory etc. I heard. I'm sorry. Believe me. Still, one door closed another opens. It's from Poland this. Best there is. To home . . . where we all belong.

Billy   It doesn't belong to me . . . Morocco.

Morocco   Of course it belongs to you. Who else can it belong to? It belongs to me. It belongs to everyone . . . to us.

Billy   You've got money, Morocco, you wouldn't understand.

Morocco   Take it from me. It's the same old place. I may have been away, but I see the old faces, smell the old smells. When you're a business traveller like me, Horse, you carry your memories everywhere with you like precious stones and every night, in hotels, on trains, in ditches, you take them out and count them, you examine every facet, you count and recount for comfort's sake till you fall asleep. Believe me your memories are more valuable than money, never mind the currency.

Horse   Is this stuff nicked?

Morocco   Never.

Berlin   Looks dodgy to me. Smuggled over the border?

Morocco   No. It's just . . . export . . . import export.

Horse   Import export? You're a fucking smuggler.

Morocco   No . . . What else is a border for?

Horse   We could get you arrested, Morocco.

Morocco *draws a line down the middle of the table. He uses the bottles and glasses etc. to demonstrate his theories.*

Morocco   This is what a border is. See . . . ?

Berlin   What?

Morocco   A magic money line. See. You pass something across it and it's suddenly worth more. Pass it across again and now it's cheaper. More . . . less . . . less . . . more . . . fags, drink, jobs, cars . . . less is more, more or less . . . see? Magic money just for crossing a magic line. I'm not a smuggler, I'm a magician, an illusionist. There's no crime in that.

Berlin   The money's real enough though, isn't it. Mr Smart Shoes. You've done well.

Again **Morocco** *demonstrates, this time he performs the trick.*

Morocco   I swear to God it's a conjuring trick. Swear to God. Give me a dollar . . . abracadabra . . . I give you roubles back . . . give me some roubles . . . come on . . . give . . . hey presto . . . Deutschmarks. It's all imaginary . . . none of it's real, none. You just have to think up the trick . . . it's easy.

Billy Maybe to you. But there has to be –

Horse A catch.

Berlin There has to be rules.

Morocco The more rules the better. The more rules there are the more people get caught in the net and the more it takes magicians to find the gaps. I need rules. I feed on them.

Billy You're a trader by your nature, Morocco.

Berlin A slippery customer.

Billy You were born to it. We're just workers.

Horse We just make stuff.

Berlin It's all we can do.

Morocco Then you're fucked. Anyone can make. Anyone. Koreans, Japs, English, anyone . . . they make. The magic comes in the buying and selling. You move something from place to place and money sticks to it . . . like a sticky sweet picks up fluff. Take it from me. I swear to God it's magic.

Horse Any cunt . . .

Berlin Any one.

Morocco You know what I mean. I'm only telling you the truth.

Berlin We got the gist, Morocco.

Horse Followed the thread.

Morocco . . . come on . . . have another one . . . have another I've got plenty.

Morocco *shares out more vodka.*

Horse So Morocco's a travelling magician . . .

Morocco At your service. Whatever you desire.

Horse Can you magic me a cock that'll piss cold beer.

Berlin   Or an arse that shits cash.

Express train passing.

8   Trainspotting

Adele *at dawn, unlocking the station doors.* **Katia** *and* **Sava** *are asleep.* **Katia** *is sitting slightly apart asleep.* **Adele** *kneels beside her, at a slight distance and looks at her. Some moments pass.*

Katia   What? What's going . . . oh . . . it's you . . . look . . . we'll be out in a minute.

Adele   I didn't think you'ld be awake. It's early.

Katia   We'll be gone in a minute . . . we'll go.

Adele   You can go back to sleep. It's not important . . . the first train's passing . . . in five minutes . . . I've come to watch.

Katia   To watch what?

Adele   I'm sorry?

Katia   What happens at five thirty in the morning?

Adele   A train passes. Vienna. I watch them from the roof.

Katia   You're trainspotting?

. . .

Adele   Have you ever been to Vienna?

Katia   No.

Adele   Budapest?

Katia   Once.

Adele   You've been!

Katia   Once. Why?

Adele   It's where the train goes. (*Consulting brochures.*) Hungary's ancient capital.

Katia   Yes.

Adele   City of contrasts.

Katia   I suppose.

Adele   Beautiful Hapsburg Buda nestling in the hills.

Katia   I don't remember.

Adele   And the glories of bustling Pest.

Katia   Yes.

Adele   What was it like?

Katia   It was nice.

Adele   Nice.

Katia   Look, we needed a place to stay.

Adele   A big hotel on the banks of the Danube.

Katia   What?

Adele   Is that where you stayed?

Katia   I mean here . . . that's why we're still here, this morning. I'm sorry if it's a problem. We stayed the night. We slept here.

Adele   Tell me more.

Katia   It was cold . . . it's a station, I suppose, not a hotel. You can't be blamed for the temperature.

Adele   Tell me more about Budapest.

Katia   It was a long time ago. I don't remember.

Adele   Was it different?

Katia   To what?

Adele   To . . . this.

Katia   Slightly. Are you going to throw us out or not?

Adele   I've read about it, imagined it, I've been there so often in my head. I think I'd recognise it. I think I'd remember it. Maybe we could go back together.

Katia   I don't know what you're talking about.

Sava   Hmmm?

Adele   Five thirty-two. Nearly time.

Sava   What's . . . going . . .

Katia   Shhh

They freeze.

Sava   Katia . . . is that . . . I thought . . .

Katia   It's nothing, Dad . . . you're dreaming.

Sava   Hmm . . .

There's a pause.

Adele   He's your father?

Katia   He's tired. We've been travelling. I'll wake him up if you want us to leave. Otherwise he needs some sleep . . .

Adele   Is your husband . . . ? Are you . . . ?

Katia   I'm not married.

Adele   But you're . . . I mean –

Katia   Nice looking girl like me? I know. Look, I'd like to chat but –

Adele   I didn't . . . mean . . . I meant. It's unusual. Isn't it? Not to be married.

Katia   Is it? Look, do you want something?

Adele   No.

Katia   You're very inquisitive.

Adele   Just a conversation.

Katia   I don't do conversation.

Adele   I only . . . I . . .

Katia   You what? What do you want?

Adele   It's just –

Katia   It's too early to work? You're not after throwing us out. So what do you want?

Adele   It's nothing special . . . I like to sit.
I like to watch the trains in the mornings, that's all.
. . .

Katia   Lovely.

Adele   The view, the forest, you can see across the town . . . that's all.

Katia   You do this every morning?

Adele   Most.

Katia   When there's a train due?

Adele   You can see it coming for miles. Out of the hills, across the fields into the forest . . . When it comes through the station you can almost touch it. Would you? You wouldn't . . . ?

Katia   I wouldn't what?

Adele   Like to. Just if you wanted.

Katia   What?

Adele   . . . come with me.

Katia   You're not going to throw us out?

Adele   No. Of course not . . . Please.

Katia   I don't know what to make of you.

Adele   Don't make anything.

Katia   Very intriguing. You're not psychotic, are you?

Adele   I . . .

Katia   Only whenever I meet intriguing women they always turn out to be crazed in some way.

Adele   I'm not what you think.

Katia   That's what they all say.

Adele (*looks at watch*)   It's nearly time.

She climbs up to the roof.

It's coming. Hurry up.

Katia *follows her.*

Katia   Is this it?

Adele   There.

Katia   I can't see anything.

Adele   It's miles away still. Watch! It'll disappear in a minute
. . . the lights get lost in the forest.

Katia *sits. It's still cold. She holds her body to keep warm.*

Katia   Christ, it's freezing out here.

Adele   It's come from Amsterdam.

Katia   I'll probably get piles.

Adele *grabs her hand and points it in the direction of the train.*

Adele   Look. Follow my hand. A chain of lights, look for a
little chain of lights . . . a chain of Amsterdam diamonds . . .

A pause. She lets go of **Katia**'s *hand and moves away slightly.*

Fret *unlocks the station door. Loudly.* **Sava** *is asleep under the blanket.
He wakes up. They look at each other.*

Fret   . . .

Sava   . . .

Fret   You're on the floor.

Adele *is staring at* **Katia**.

Katia   Please don't gaze at me.

Adele   Sorry.

Sava   Sorry . . . we eh . . . stayed.

Fret   I'll have to sweep it now. My floor.

Sava   Yes.

Fret   That one.

Sava *looks about him.*

Fret   The one you're on.

Katia   You can look if you want. But I can't bear gazing.

Adele   Sorry.

Sava   I'll get up right away.

Fret   You will.

Sava   Just now.

Fret   Yes.

Sava (*groans*)   I can see my breath in front of me, it's so cosy under the blanket. I hate getting up in the winter, don't you?

Fret   I'm sorry?

Sava   I was just saying –

Fret   I don't think I wanted to banter. Did I look like I wanted to banter?

Sava   No.

Fret   Right.

Fret *goes into his office.* **Sava** *gets up quickly and bundles up his blanket.*

Katia   You're doing it again?

Adele   I wasn't, I was looking for the train.

Fret *emerges from his office with a brush. He holds it as though it was a weapon of defence.*

Sava   You know, you might be ill.

Fret   What?

Sava   You seem edgy. Upset, sarcasm, nerves. You look terrible. Perhaps you've got acid in the stomach. They're classic symptoms.

Fret   Perhaps I'm just nervous, sarcastic and upset. The symptoms are the same. It's hard to tell.

Katia   I'm not a tropical fish.

Sava *takes the brush.*

Sava   I'll give you a hand if you like.

Fret   Thank you.

Sava *begins to sweep.* **Fret** *inspects the timetables and tries to work out when the trains are due today. He is about to write them down on the blackboard.*

Adele   Where do you come from?

Katia   Does it matter?

Adele   I'm only asking.

Katia   I'm not sure.

Adele   Not sure?

Katia   Like I said. I'm not sure.

Adele   But. You must know. Everyone knows where they come from.

Katia   The place I came from isn't there any more. It disappeared.

Adele   A place can't just disappear.

Katia   Its name was taken off the maps and signposts. I couldn't find it anywhere.

Adele   Its name might have changed but the place must still be there. It's the same place . . . isn't it?

Katia   There's no way of checking.

Fret   You – you're waiting for a train, aren't you?

Sava   Well . . .

Fret (*he points to the timetables*)   These – rubbish. Meaningless rubbish.

Sava   Timetables are always difficult to follow.

Fret   You try. Go on, imagine you're a passenger.

Sava   I see.

Fret   OK. Imagine you want to travel from here to here overnight.

Sava   From where . . . here? . . . Right.

Fret   Now ordinarily you change trains here, in this station. Just after passport control at the border. Then you'd wait for one of the slow local trains in the morning.

Sava   I see. What do you want to know?

Fret   Imagine that's the journey. What would you do?

Adele   Maybe I can help. I've a map of Europe. What was it called, the town?

Katia   It had a number of names. None of them stuck.

Adele   What did it look like? Big, small . . . what?

Katia   It looked like a small town. The sort of place people come from. Not the sort of place they go to, particularly.

Sava   Aha! A knife and fork. Does that mean I can use the buffet?

Fret   Restaurant car. Only for first-class ticket holders.

Sava   Oh. But overnight I'd want to eat.

Fret   You can pack banana sandwiches.

Sava   Well, I think I would take the international express to Sofia which goes through Wroclaw . . . change there . . . now there's a wait I think . . .

Adele   Perhaps . . . if you know what it looked like . . . that would be a clue.

Katia   I didn't recognise it the last time I saw it. Its appearance had changed considerably. It was difficult to tell if it was the same place. I had to ask a policeman.

Adele   What did he say?

Katia   He said he didn't know. He was from somewhere else. He was new to the place himself.

Adele   Didn't you recognise anything?

Katia   At midday the place was still. Everyone was indoors to escape the sun. I stood on the street kicking dust and listening to insects. The feeling of stillness. I recognised that. Apart from the stillness I could see nothing that I knew. Nothing familiar.

Adele   How had it changed?

Katia   It reminded me of a relative whose face has been torn off.

Adele   You think I'm ignorant. Don't you?

Sava   Now is it Friday?

Fret   It's not Friday.

Sava   So it's not a starred day and we've agreed I don't need a sleeper carriage. Let me see now.

Adele   I know about where you're from. I know about the war. I know about all that. I read the papers. I asked a question from simple human curiosity . . . I want to know you. I want to know about you. I've not been very far in my life, I've not travelled, not like you. But I'm not ignorant. You don't have to humour me.

Adele *starts to go.*

Katia   What about your train?

Adele   It'll be there tomorrow.

Katia   Wait.
Please.
I'm sorry. I was being rude and defensive.
I can't help it. I said I wasn't good at conversation.
Please stay.

Adele   The war must have affected you. I understand.

Katia   Oh no. I was rude and defensive before the war. The war just gave me a chance to practice.

Adele   Quiet!

Katia   What?

Adele   Listen.

Katia   What?

Adele   Listen. You're not listening. Stay still.

Katia   The train?

Adele   It's coming out of the forest. It's getting nearer.

Katia   What do we do now?

Adele   We wait.

Katia   You certainly know how to show a girl a good time, Adele.

Sava   I don't think it can be done, Mr Fret.

Fret   See! It makes no sense.

Sava   I think this station's closed.

Fret   Exactly. It's rubbish. Balls.

Sava   Here, you see. In small writing. This station's marked with an x.

Fret (*reading*)   'Station no longer in operation.'

Sava   I think you are, Mr Fret.

Fret   What?

Sava No Longer Operative as of . . . next month.

Fret No. No.

Adele I'm glad you came to watch. I didn't think. Someone like you – You're not bored, are you?

Katia Bored, no.

Adele Only I don't often meet foreigners. The trains are full of them, obviously, but they usually don't bother to get off. No one stops here. I just wanted to make friends.

Katia Friends are like children, they're fine when they're other people's, but I wouldn't want any of my own.

Adele Sometimes they just happen to you.

Sava It says here you can take the bus from Lezno.

Fret A bus! A bus! How can a grown man take the bus with any dignity. Sitting with students and chickens, yobs and failures.

Adele Quarter to six, it's nearly time . . . any minute. Come on.

Sava I understand how you must feel.

Fret Do you?

Sava I said before. I worked on the railways as well. I understand.

Adele It creeps up on you. You'll feel it soon in your feet.

Fret I don't understand it at all. It makes no sense to me.

Adele And then your legs. You'll feel it come closer.

Fret Since they opened the border the trains don't have to stop here any more.

Adele You can feel the concrete shake.

Fret It used to be we had a customs post here and pass control and everything. Now they do all that in between stops. The border doesn't mean much when you're on a train. So long as your pass is checked somewhere in between . . . it's more efficient.

Katia   I can hear it. I can hear it now.

Fret   I said to them. Don't expect me to stand in the way of change. I'm all for it. I'm a railwayman. I'm all for progress.

Adele   And now the horn . . . any second.

A train horn in the distance.

Fret   I'm all for going forward. Things have to get better. Machines get bigger, smoother, the engineering safer. I'm all for efficiency.

Adele   Thirty coaches long, the carriages at the front are from Holland, then some German, some from Poland. Tonnes and tonnes of steel. Wood and glass –

The noise is building up.

Fret   So now they tell me this. Thirty years of progress, thirty years of laying down tracks and making trains and they send me this.

Sava   I understand.

Adele   Now the lights. See . . . you can see in at the people in the carriages . . . sitting, smoking, reading papers . . . ever since I was small I've stood up here to watch . . . a train full of everything. Every kind of thing from everywhere's inside it. Everything from everywhere is on that train and it's coming through here . . . stay still. (*She's shouting now.*) Hold still and feel it . . . can you feel it? Can you feel it . . .

The train's noise is at its peak. The train passes.

Act Two

9 The Second Chorus

1 & **2** *are women.*

1 Autumn's arrived in our town,

2 changing the colour of the forest,

3 bringing rain,

4 bringing wolves.

5 On the plains, at the heart of Europe,

6 we build fires,

7 strip fields,

8 and make soup.

1 But, late at night,

2 at the forest's end,

3 where the housing blocks sit in mud,

4 at the edge of the town,

5 wolves move among the bins,

6 dragging black sacks into the dark like killed deer.

7 Men stand at the bar counter and complain.

Men We never got wolves before,

8 before they hid in the woods all winter,

3 now they sniff around the shadows at the bottom of the stairwell.

1 Smoke and the smell of beer hangs over the men.

2 Their voices creep out onto the dark street,

4   what's happened to this place?

5   I don't recognise it any more.

6   Maybe we lost it in a game of cards.

7   Maybe it disappeared into the forest.

8   Maybe it was stolen while our backs were turned.

All   Only it isn't our place any more.

1   Our place was taken in the night.

8   Our place slipped away while we were asleep.

10   Conversation

Adele and **Berlin**. *The television is on. Brochures lie around the floor.* **Adele** *has a pencil and paper and is writing down information.*

Berlin   Switch it off.

Adele   It's the holiday programme.

Berlin   I want to talk.

Adele   She's going to France this week and –

Berlin   I don't give a fuck.

Adele   To Marseilles.

Berlin   Switch if off.

Adele   I'm watching it.

Berlin *switches television off. This has obviously happened before.*

Berlin   Fucking France fucking Spain . . . you watch too much TV. Too much utter crap. I want to talk. We used to talk. We had proper conversations. We spoke to each other . . . remember? I said words and you replied to them. It's what a wife's supposed to do. It's part of the job.

Adele   . . .

Berlin   You're rusty, obviously. I'll start. How about this –
why don't you sleep with me any more?

Adele   . . .

Berlin   Try again. I don't think you've got the hang. I ask
you a question and then you think of what the answer is . . .
then you say it and that's how it starts . . . a chat. So here we
go . . . why don't you sleep with me any more?

Adele   . . .

Berlin   You have to say, I don't know, something maybe
like –

Adele   It's because you disgust me.

Berlin   . . .

Adele   You disgust me. Like a corpse would. Turns my
stomach to touch you . . . it's not your fault. I live in a
graveyard, I was bound to marry a stiff. Don't be shocked. I
thought you wanted a chat. Not chatty? Why not say
something like . . . how about . . . 'Adele, how can you say
that,' or 'Adele'.

Berlin   If I could . . . I . . . If I could I'd take you to
whatever fucking seaside town you want. You could have
window seats on the Orient Express. If I could I'd buy you a
frigging flight across Persia on a magic carpet . . . But I don't
have a job any more. It's how things are. Terrible.

Adele   Nothing's 'how it is'.

Berlin   What is it you think you want, Adele?

Adele   Forget it, it's not you . . . There's nothing you can do
about it. It's me . . . being here. I feel like I'm being buried
every time I look at you. Every time I remember where I am
it's like a fistful of earth falls on my face. I need to get some
air, have to dig myself out.

Berlin   I can help.

Adele   You can't.

Berlin   Why not?

Adele   Because you've got no imagination. I live in the
world, Berlin. A world with millions of things in. But not you.
You're here. If you can't see it it doesn't exist. If it's over the
horizon no one lives there.

Berlin   I've got my feet planted. There's nothing wrong
with that. Got my heels dug in. It makes you stronger.

. . .

Let's not argue about it now.

He lamely attempts to kiss her.

Adele   I'm going out.

Berlin   Where to?

Adele   To the station.

Berlin   Why?

Adele   Don't wait up.

Berlin   You've got it wrong again, Adele. This isn't how
conversation goes. You've missed the whole idea.

Adele   Bye.

Berlin   I'll wait for you . . . we'll have another conversation!
Tonight. Another talk . . . I'll be here. Adele . . . We can make
it a regular thing . . . Adele!

Express train passing.

11   Points

Fret *and* **Sava** *are on the roof.* **Katia** *and* **Adele** *are in the main
hall.*

Adele   You'll like him.

Katia   How do you know?

Adele   Because I know. He's one of us.

Katia   What's one of us?

Adele   I mean he's . . . cosmopolitan. There's not a place in Europe Morocco hasn't seen.

Fret   The points there – you see . . . pre-war. I have to operate them manually.

Sava   At least with manual points you know where you are. With automated points you haven't a clue what's going on.

Fret   You've no control.

Sava   It's a disaster waiting to happen.

Fret   That's what I said. It's what I said to head office.

Sava   I'd say it myself. If I was in your shoes.

Katia   Is he reliable?

Adele   Reliable?

Katia   Will he turn us in?

Adele   I don't think so.

Katia   I don't like you telling people.

Adele   I don't see why I should keep you a secret.

Katia   I'm not supposed to be here.

Adele   Neither am I.

Katia   I'm undesirable.

Adele   I don't think so.

Katia   Everyone else does.

Fret   If they close the station, who's going to operate the points?

Sava   A computer operator in the capital. An oily suit in an office.

Fret   Exactly. A college boy.

Sava   Who's never had his hands on a piece of dirty metal in his life.

Fret   Who's never got up at six to stand at the trackside and wait for the express . . . six hundred lives in your hands on an autumn morning.

Sava   There's something spiritual about it.

Fret   Spiritual. Exactly.

Sava   Almost religious.

Fret   When it comes to manual points I'm orthodox. I'm a fundamentalist.

The noise of the train in the distance coming nearer.

Sava   Look, here she comes . . . see.

Fret   Beautiful. Listen . . . sshhh!

Sava   I can hear.

Fret   The sound of machinery running smoothly . . . gorgeous.

Sava   A hymn. The sound of it. A hymn to engineering.

Adele   Why can't you stay here?

Katia   They say we're economic migrants.

Adele   That's terrible. Are you?

Katia   Who knows. Economics is a big subject.

Sava   It's a funny thing, Mr Fret, but in my experience a railwayman is a railwayman wherever you go. We speak the same language, we think the same way.

Fret   When I was a boy, I saw them laying the first tracks into the town. Tracks and sleepers. Gangs of men handling the steel and blocks.

Sava   Tito was a railwayman. My father was a railwayman.

Fret   I said to myself. That's what Europe will be. Steel and tracks and trains.

Sava   I'm a railwayman, you're a railwayman.

Fret   Steel and tracks and trains like blood muscle and arteries holding the continent together. Connecting this place with a hundred thousand other places like it from Rotterdam to Athens.

Sava   For all I know God's a railwayman.

Fret   If God was a railwayman then things would stay on track. Things would run smoothly. I'd say God works in head office. I'd say God wears a suit.

Adele   Morocco will know what to do. He'll know.

Katia   Why are you helping me? What's in it for you?

Adele   Nothing. You.

Katia   Me?

Adele   I mean . . . I'd like to come with you.

Katia   You belong here. What do you need me for?

Adele   Europe.
I want you to show me around.

Katia   You should be happy with what you've got. Stay where you fit in. Stay at home. You're lucky you've got one. I've got nothing.

Adele   But . . . you've seen things, you've travelled, I've only imagined .

Katia   Whatever you can imagine for yourself, Adele, this continent can come up with much worse. You'll soon learn the best way is to stay where you are, keep quiet and lie low. Believe me, you're better off where you belong.

Adele   But travel broadens the mind. That's what they say . . . Isn't it?

Katia   Well, they're wrong. It doesn't broaden the mind, it stretches it like skin across a tanning rack . . . a pegged skin out to dry. Each thing you see, each thing the continent coughs up for you stretches it tighter until you can't keep all the things you've seen in the same mind and the skin rips down the middle.

Morocco *arrives*.

Morocco   Someone's telling travellers' tales. Can I join in?

Adele   Morocco! You came!

Morocco   Of course.

Adele   Where have you been?

Morocco   Everywhere, across the border, down south, up north all around . . . and I've brought presents . . . look . . . dollars, marks . . . Swiss francs . . . French francs . . . the lot. And I went to Vienna.

Adele   I told you he was cosmopolitan. What was it like?

Morocco   It was all right. Who's your friend?

Adele   She's a traveller. What happened in Vienna?

Morocco   I met a woman.

Adele   Tell me more.

Morocco   What sort of traveller?

Katia   What business is it of yours?

Adele   Tell me about the woman.

Morocco   We made love. I might be able to help you.

Katia   What makes you think I need help?

Adele   Everyone loves Morocco.

Morocco (*to* **Katia**)   It's my nose.

Adele   Your nose?

Morocco   I can smell need.

Adele   What was she like?

Morocco   She was strawberry blonde with red-rimmed glasses.

Katia   What does your nose tell you about me?

Adele   Tell me more.

Katia   You need papers and a place to stay.

Adele   Tell me about the woman.

Morocco   She was hard.
It was like getting blood out of a stone.
She said I could only touch her here.

He demonstrates by putting his hand on **Katia**. **Katia** *lets it happen. A bargain is being struck.*

Morocco   Of course I ignored her. I'm very persistent. A good negotiator . . . I don't take no for an answer.

Katia   Can you get me papers?

Morocco   Perhaps. It depends.

Adele   How far did you go?

Morocco   I went all the way.

Katia   Do you want money?

Morocco   Money? I don't like money, you never know what it's worth. I'm a trader. I deal in things.

Katia   What things?

Morocco   It depends. I have to use my nose again. I can also smell an opportunity.

Katia   You have a very adaptable nose.

Morocco   It's my flexible friend.

Adele   The woman – how did you seduce her . . . what did you do?

Morocco (*he demonstrates on* **Katia**)   At first when I touched her she slapped my hand and put it back.

Adele   And then?

Morocco   I tried again. I was insistent.

Adele   And then?

Morocco   And then my hand stayed put. We . . . negotiated.

Adele   He negotiated. So cosmopolitan. So civilized.

Morocco   I can't bargain on an empty stomach. Let's eat. I know a little place in town. It's a well-kept secret. I'm a friend of the manager. I'm sure he'll take good care of us. I have my own table.

Adele   He has a table.

Morocco   The Calypso Bar. I'll be there at eight.

Katia   So will I.

Morocco   I look forward to it. It'll be a special night.

Morocco *leaves.*

Sava   I ought to thank you.

Fret   Ought you?

Sava   For letting us stay. I ought to.

Fret   You know . . . it's uncommon . . . in this day and age.

Sava   It is?

Fret   It's rare . . . these days. To meet a colleague. Such as yourself. Who understands. It's uncommon.

Sava   I – we understand trains, that's all.

Fret   I'm not a sentimental man. I'm practical. Perhaps you haven't felt welcome. I'm sorry for that.

Sava   I like a little hostility. It puts me at my ease.

Fret   I've enjoyed . . . these past few weeks. Your staying here.

Sava   It's been a privilege.

Fret   Adele doesn't care for running a station. She hasn't the commitment. You've been a help.

Sava   It was my pleasure. Please. As one comrade – if I can use that word – to another . . . it was a pleasure.

Fret   When the station closes you'll have to leave.

Sava   Perhaps the station needn't close.

Fret   It's too late now. Things have gone too far.

Sava   Maybe not. We could protest.

Fret   I thought protest only made things worse.

Sava   In the yards at Knin we did it once. We staged a sit-in.

Fret   Did you get what you wanted?

Sava   No.

Fret   See.

Sava   It didn't matter. What we wanted wasn't important. We made them notice. We annoyed them.

Fret   A sit-in.

Sava   It's worth trying.

Fret   I suppose when you get to our age a sit-in is the only kind of defiance you've got the energy left for. In the office I've got comfortable chairs and there's plenty coffee. We could hold out for weeks.

Katia   The Warsaw train's coming.

Adele   I know.

Katia   Don't you want to go and see? I thought you . . .

Adele   Do you?

Katia   No.

Adele   Neither do I.

Adele   Tell me something.

Katia   What?

Adele   Anything . . . something about you.

Katia   No.

Adele   Tell me what you've seen.

Katia   No.

Adele   Tell me . . . tell me your life story.

Katia   I don't have a life story. I'm one of the few people left who doesn't.

Adele   Why not?

Katia   I'm a traditionalist, I like my stories to have a point.

Adele   Tell me what happened to you . . . ?

Katia   Why?

Adele   I'm interested . . .

Katia   I'm not a tourist brochure. I'm not for browsing.

A pause.

Adele   I want to kiss you.

Katia   Why?

Adele   To taste.

They kiss.

Katia   What did you taste?

Adele   Forest.

Katia   I forgot to pack my toothbrush.

Adele   Foreign languages.

Katia   I've drunk coffee.

Adele   Smoke.

Katia   It's a terrible habit – what do you want, Adele?

Adele   Nothing . . .
You.
Everything.

She moves to kiss her again.

Katia   Don't.

They kiss.

The train noise is building incessantly.

Sava   Here it comes. Here it comes . .

Fret   Magnificent . . . no orchestra could sound better.

Sava   No singer could be smoother.

Fret   It's a masterpiece. It's a bloody European classic.

They can barely be heard. Express train passes.

12   Departure

*The bus stop. **Billy** is leaving. He sits with his bag at his feet. **Horse** and **Berlin** are sitting with him. It's cold. **Horse** is writing 'foreigners out' on the bus stop.*

Billy   . . . do you have to do that? Someone might see.

Horse   That's the idea.

Berlin   You can't stop him. He's very zealous. The zeal of the convert. If you stand still long enough he'll write 'foreigners out' on your forehead.

Horse   It isn't you who should be leaving, Billy. Leaving home. Forced out. You shouldn't have to go.

Billy   I'm going because I want to.

Horse   You've been driven out. You're not the only one. A lot of good men are going.

Billy   I'm going to look for work.

Horse   They give all the jobs to the Somalis and the Ethiopians. It's true.

Billy   Who's 'they', Horse?

Horse   The left.

Berlin   The dirty anarchists. The Jews and the gyppos. The blacks and the browns.

Billy   I see.

Berlin   Polluters of the nation.

Horse   We didn't used to have them, Billy, there didn't used to be foreigners here. Now we've blocks full of them. Five to a room.

Berlin   They're bound to breed. Like rats in the damp.

Billy   You should know better, Berlin.

Berlin   Better than what?

Billy   Better than to go to these meetings. Listen to that shit.

Berlin   It keeps me off the streets. Besides I like it.

Billy   Why?

Berlin   Because it's dumb.

Billy   Berlin.

Berlin   It's dumb and blunt. Because it's beautiful. Because it's better than church.

Billy   You don't believe it any more than I do. You know it's not true.

Berlin   I like believing in things that aren't true. That's what faith is.

Billy   What about the violence?

Berlin   All necessary means in defence of the faith.

Billy   Right.

Berlin   Right.

Horse   Let's not argue. Not on Billy's last day.

Berlin   I'm not arguing.

Billy   You're spouting shite.

Berlin   Fuck you.

Horse   Come on.

Berlin   What?

Horse   Don't fight. Let's not fight. We're mates. We're pals. Pals don't fight. Come on.

Berlin   Pals. Aye. Right enough. Pals.

A pause.

Billy   Funny to be leaving. Never thought I'd –

Berlin   Things change.

Billy   Aye. Things change.

Horse   They don't have to change.

Billy   Still. Off to the smoke. Make my fortune and that.

Berlin   You'll be a rich man.

Billy   Drive a Volvo.

Berlin   A Mercedes.

Billy   Black windows.

Berlin   A bar in the back.

Horse   You can give us lifts.

Billy   I'll buy you one of your own.

Berlin   You'll be a rich man.

Billy   You wait. One day. I'll drive up this road. And you'll all come out and say, 'Who's this? Who's this rich guy coming here? Who's in the car?' And I'll wind down the window.

Berlin   Electric.

Horse   Zzzzzzzzz.

Billy   Hello. I'm back, boys. Fancy a drink.

Horse   I've come to buy the factory.

Berlin   I've come to do the business.

Billy   The factory's fucked. (*A pause.*)
I'm buying a mansion. A dacha in the country.

Berlin   Aye, right.

Horse   A dacha?

Berlin   In the country?

Horse   Billy, I . . .

Billy   Look . . . I hate goodbyes can we just . . . I'll . . . send
you a . . .

Berlin   Aye, do that . . .

Horse   . . .
. . . a postcard?

Billy   Yeah. A postcard. From . . . wherever.

Berlin   A card from wherever.

Horse   From where?

Billy   You know . . . wherever I happen to get to.

Berlin   You never know where he'll get to.

Billy   You're right enough there . . . follow the old nose,
that's me.

Horse   Remember we're still here if you . . . you know.

Billy   It's not easy . . . the right words and all that. You don't
have to wait you know. Bus'll be here anytime. It's freezing.

Horse   Fucking is as well.

Berlin   Picked a day for it.

Horse *shakes* **Billy***'s hand.*

All   Certainly picked a day for it.

Billy *goes to shake hands with* **Berlin**. *They pause. There is embarrassment. They withdraw.*

Berlin   That's the bus coming. Got your ticket?

Billy   . . .
thanks for . . .

Berlin   No problem.

Billy   I'll just go then . . . I hate –

Berlin   You go then.

Horse   Bus is here.

Billy *picks up his bag . . . leaves for bus.*

Billy   Cheers then.

Both   . . . Cheers.

Leaves.

Billy *waves. Reluctant to go.* **Berlin** *and* **Horse** *wave.*

Horse   I think I'll miss him, Berlin. He's a good man. Billy. Place'll be different without him.

Berlin   I won't be different, it'll be the same.

Horse   . . . with Billy gone though.

Berlin   Place'll be the same. A turd drying up in the sun.

The sound of a bus pulling away.

13   Community issues

Adele *and* **Katia** *in the waiting room.* **Sava** *and* **Fret** *are on the station roof. The station is now hung with banners of protest. 'Stop the closure', 'Save our station' and* **Sava** *is engaged in painting 'Trains not . . .' Both men are drinking bottles of* **Morocco**'s *vodka.*

Katia   What time is it?

Adele   I don't know.

Katia   What time is it?

Adele   I don't care.

Katia   Adele.

Adele   I want you.

Katia *grabs her wrist to look at her watch.*

Katia   Be serious. Twenty past seven.

She lets go of **Adele**. **Adele** *remains waiting, her eyes half-closed.*

Katia   I've got forty minutes.

Sava   Fret?

Fret   What?

Sava   What rhymes with trains?

Fret   . . . Brains . . . Cranes . . . Drains . . .

Sava   No, it has to be something we don't want . . . Trains not . . . um . . .

Fret   . . . Lanes?

Sava   Lanes?

Fret   As in . . . motorway . . . lanes.

Sava   I don't think so.

Fret   Trains not – does it have to rhyme?

Sava   It's no use having a slogan if it doesn't rhyme. No one'll take you seriously.

Fret   It hardly seems to matter.

Sava   It does. It's like a good acronym. You have to have one if you're going to protest in this day and age. Without an acronym, a rhyming slogan and a concerned actress you'll be ignored.

Fret   Haven't you noticed?

Sava   What?

Fret   We're supposed to be protesters and no one's turned up. The trains have stopped stopping. The change has taken place. On the quiet. Without ceremony. There's no one out there . . . no audience, no officials . . . no one but the wolves to read the slogans. So it doesn't matter whether it rhymes or not. Does it?

Sava   It matters to me. Literary integrity. That sort of thing. I don't mind if anyone's listening. It gives me pleasure for it to be said properly. That's enough.

Katia   Show me where the Calypso Bar is. Draw me a map.

Adele   I'll take you.

Katia   It's business.

Adele   You're getting fake papers? You're moving on. Morocco told me. I'm in the know.

Katia   So what.

Adele   I've got papers too. Let me travel with you.

Katia   No.

Adele   Why not?

Katia   I don't need extra baggage. I'm going alone.

Adele   We could be travelling companions. The two of us . . .

Katia   It's not the grand tour.

Adele   We could jump the trains together. We could fuck in the toilets when the conductor passes.

Katia   Use your brain, Adele.

Adele   I am. I'm using my imagination.

Katia   We fucked once.

Adele   Twice.

Katia   You've got some sort of pathetic crush on me, that's all.

Adele   Katia.

Katia   We fucked. Maybe we shouldn't have. Maybe I should have left you alone. But we fucked. It was something to do while I waited for a train.

. . .

I owe you nothing. People fuck all the time. It means nothing.

Adele   Yes.

Katia   Just forget it. For God's sake don't turn it into a tragedy.

Adele   No.

Katia   I don't belong here. I have to get out. You live here. It's your place.

Adele   Yes.

Katia   I like you, Adele. It might surprise you but I like you.

Adele   Good.

Katia   God knows why.

Adele   God knows.

Katia   Things happen between people. Things happen and then they stop. Like a summer cold. Trains pass. You can't just attach yourself to someone and leave. You can't do it. Your place is here, Adele. Believe me. I know.

Long pause.

Adele   I was born here by mistake. I didn't choose it. It happened to me.
Like a car accident.
You think you know me but you don't. You don't know the first thing about me.
I'm not what you think I am, Katia.
You've never seen me before.

Katia No.

Adele You've lost your home and I've never had one. So we're both exiles.

. . .

Besides. I don't need to ask you. I only asked you out of politeness. I'll come anyway. I'll follow you anyway. You won't lose me.

Katia You're very persistent.

Adele You're very stubborn.

Katia I don't want a puppy. If I wanted a puppy I'd buy one. You'ld have to look after yourself.

Adele I already do.

Katia It would be your problem if you got into trouble.

Adele It always is.

Katia It's not Club Med.

Adele I don't expect Club Med.

Katia Just don't expect anything, Adele. Don't imagine things'll be like anything . . . don't expect anything except rain and policemen and stinking suburbs that look the same wherever you are.

Adele I expect nothing.

Berlin *has arrived. Unnoticed.*

Katia I have to go. I've got to meet Morocco.

Adele Will you come back here later?

Katia I don't have anywhere else to go . . .

Adele Katia . . .

They kiss. Uneasily. Not yet resolved. **Katia** *notices* **Berlin**. *She leaves.* **Berlin** *lets her pass.*

Adele You.

Berlin   Me.

Adele   What do you want?

Berlin   Where's Fret?

Adele   He's on the roof. Protesting.

Berlin   About what?

Adele   About the station.

Berlin   It's a bit late for that, isn't it? It's been weeks since a train stopped here.

Adele   It keeps him happy. What's going on, Berlin?

Berlin   Where's your friend gone, Adele?

Adele   I don't know what you're talking about.

Berlin   FRET!

Adele   What's going on?

Berlin *almost accidently kicks some of* **Katia**'*s things.*

Berlin   Things have got a bit cluttered in here.

Adele   What?

Berlin   Messy. You know. Litter. Rubbish.

Adele   Where?

Berlin   Here . . . there and everywhere. Look . . . the floor . . . the station unkempt . . . just look out at the square . . . pride of the town it used to be.

Adele   You're losing me.

Berlin   Do you remember how people used to stroll in the sunshine? Drink coffee outdoors . . . watch the world go by everything neat, everything in order.

Adele   So? . . .

Berlin   Look at it now.

Adele   It's nearly winter. No one's going to sit outdoors.

Berlin   Grass verges untended. The road left pot-holed and crumbling at the edges . . . Vagrants under the trees . . . strange faces at the bar counter.

Adele   Berlin?

Berlin   I've got time on my hands, Adele. I notice the little things.

Adele   Is this you and Horse . . . is this your little group?

Berlin   I want to discuss community issues . . . that's all . . . A bit of tidying up we want done. We've had a meeting. It's been agreed.

Adele   Who, Berlin? Who?

Berlin   The community. FRET!

Adele   Which community? I wasn't there.

Fret enters. **Horse** *has appeared behind* **Sava** *and suddenly grabs him, covering his mouth. He begins to punch the older man in the stomach and face methodically and quietly.*

Berlin   There you are, Fret.

Fret   What do you want?

Berlin   I'm here on behalf of a . . . on behalf of the community, Fret. To hand over a petition . . . we've all signed it . . . People are frightened, Fret, frightened and upset.

Fret   Are they?

Berlin   Because when they pass their once beloved old station they find it's been turned into some sort of hostel for the homeless.

Fret   The station's closed. You'ld think people would be concerned about that.

Berlin   Not just vagrancy, Fret, but prostitutes seem to be operating out of here. Gypsy prostitutes. It's not on, Fret. It's affecting the women.

Fret   The station's shut. No longer in operation.

Berlin   I think we're all sorry about that, Fret. Like I said, I've brought a petition. Just to say . . . well . . . If they're not gone soon . . .

Fret   Get out.

Berlin   I probably don't have to tell you that there's unruly elements in the town . . . you know . . . hotheads etc. I hate to be the bringer of bad news but . . .

Fret   Is this a threat? I'll call the police.

Sava *has gone limp.* **Horse** *lets him drop. He stands above him holding his fist which is now sore. He sucks his fist.*

Horse   You cunt.

Berlin   Do.

Horse   Bloody old hard-boned cunt.

Berlin   Do that.

Horse   Hurt my fist.

Horse *gives* **Sava** *a desultory kick, then leaves.*

Berlin   I wouldn't want something as worrying as this to pass them by unnoticed . . . only you know as well as I do that these people don't take a warning. They get fuelled up and there's no stopping them. I'm just saying –

Fret   What?

Berlin   I'm just saying that . . . it worries me. I'm worried.

Fret   Not sleeping?

Berlin   I suggest you tell your friends . . . for their own safety as much as anything.

Fret   You concern yourself with your friends and I'll worry about mine.

Berlin   Good.

Fret   Like I said, the station's closed.

Berlin   Well, then, bad deed done, tale told, time to go. I'll see you at home, Adele.

Adele   I don't think so.

Berlin   Later then.

Adele   I think I'm staying here tonight.

Berlin   Right . . . later then.

Express train passing.

14   Local songs

Inside the Calypso Bar. As before, **Morocco** *is sitting with* **Katia.** **Morocco** *has been drinking. We can hear a group of men singing nationalist songs in the meeting room.*

Morocco   I pity them. Locals. I pity them. They're like dogs whose owners died . . . hungry dogs lying across their masters' grave and whining to the night . . . they stay in one cold spot and wait to starve. I pity them.

Katia   I think we ought to go . . .

Morocco   Whereas yourself . . . you and me . . . I think –

Katia   Finish your drink . . . we'll go outside.

Morocco   I think we're familiar with bigger things than these louts. We're familiar with cities. We've crossed borders. We're at home only when we're away from home Here . . . we'll have a toast . . . to leaving home . . .

Katia   Will you quiet down.

Morocco   To refugees. That stuff you said about losing your home . . . you were lucky. It was a blessed release . . . nothing's more of a prison than a home. Nothing is a bigger threat to a man's liberty than three meals a day and familiar faces at the dinner table. To Freedom!

Berlin *has entered from where songs are being sung and observes the scene. While* **Katia** *speaks,* **Morocco** *is kissing her hand.*

Katia   Don't mistake me, Morocco. I'm not a trader or a traveller by nature. I'm a coward. The way you see my eyes glance is me checking the exits. I'm not a free spirit.

Morocco   Yes you are . . . You're like the breeze . . . you move like a dancer.

Katia   I fidget. I try not to give snipers a chance to set their sights. (*Indicating a roomful of singers.*)
I would like to leave now.

Morocco   Like love, you never stay too long in one place.

Katia   If I seem in a hurry to leave it's because people who stay too long in one place get noticed. People who get noticed get punished.

Songs of the men build up.

Express train passing.

15   This is nice

Adele *on the station roof. She is reading her brochures.* **Berlin** *arrives noticeably drunk.*

Berlin   Do you know what time it is?

Adele   . . .

Berlin   You're supposed to be at home.

Adele   I'm here.

Berlin   I was worried. I've been worried about you.

Adele   Why?

Berlin   Something could have happened to you. Anything could have happened. I was worried.

Adele   Go home, Berlin. I'm waiting for someone.

Berlin   It's past midnight. Who are you waiting for at this time? The trains have stopped.

Adele   Fuck you.

Berlin   Who?

Adele   Just someone.

Berlin   Maybe they'll be late.

Adele   What?

Berlin   Who you're waiting for? Maybe they've been held up.

Adele   Maybe.

Berlin   Maybe they've been delayed . . .

Adele   Berlin?

Berlin   I told you . . . anything can happen.
I don't like to worry you but it's the way things are at the moment.
Terrible.

Adele   What are you talking about?

Berlin   Who knows.

Adele   Where have you been tonight?

Berlin   Out with some mates.

Adele   Where? Out where?

Berlin   In town.

Adele   There isn't an 'in town' here, Berlin, there's the Calypso and the street.

Berlin   We were in town.

Adele   You've torn your jeans.

Berlin   That was careless.

Adele   They were new.

Berlin   Trust a woman to notice.

Adele   Your shirt.

Berlin   Stop nagging, Adele, you're not my mother.

Adele   There's spots of blood.

Berlin   Boys will be boys. We were out on the town we weren't collecting for charity.

Adele   Thought you'ld hit her, like you hit her dad?

Berlin   She oughtn't to be out so late. It's risky.

Adele   Who?

Berlin   Who?

Adele   Who oughtn't be out so late?

Berlin   Nobody. Anybody . . . everybody.

Adele   You said she.

Berlin   Did I? Come on. Come home with me. Let's get home.

Adele   Don't touch me.

Berlin   We just got a bit pissed.
She was in the alley.
She was fucking Morocco in the alley by the Calypso.
Like a dog.
Disgusting.

Adele   What did you do to her?

Berlin   Nothing.

Adele   Tell me.

Berlin   We just got a bit pissed. That's all. He wanted a fight as much as us. It was disgusting, fucking gypsies in a back alley. This town needs cleaning up. Billy was right. It's going under.

Adele   Tell me what you did.

Berlin   We gave Morocco a doing.

Adele   You –

Berlin It's a boys' thing. I knew you wouldn't
understand.

Adele . . .

A very tense pause. **Adele***'s anger is so great that she can't speak. She
can't move, she's immobilised.*

Berlin I'm sorry.
I said sorry.
What else can I say? It's done now . . . he'll be all right. It was
just a gesture. I'll speak to him in the morning. In the
morning, I'll have a word . . . sort it out. He'll be all right
about it. I know Morocco. He knows it wasn't personal.
. . .
We need to talk, Adele.
We should talk.
Adele.

Adele . . .

Berlin . . . it feels to me like you've been . . . distant . . .
lately. Somewhere else.

Adele . . .

Berlin I can't seem to get through. I can't seem to make a
connection.

Adele . . .

Berlin I'm not as bad as you think, Adele. I'm not like
Horse, I'm not like the other guys. I can feel it when there's a
problem between us. I can sense it.

Adele Go home, Berlin.

Berlin I just want to say something.

Adele Go home before I push you on the track.

Berlin This is important.

Adele I'm not listening.

He holds her.

Berlin   But you have to listen. I have to tell you . . . (*She struggles a little, he pauses, he waits till she is still before saying:*) I love you.

Adele   Berlin.

Berlin   Kiss me.

Adele   Let go of me.

Berlin   I'm worried about you . . .
We need to talk.
I don't want to let go of you . . .

Adele   Getoff.

Berlin   I feel as though if I let go I could lose you. I want to squeeze you tight. I love you, Adele, I don't want you to leave.

Adele   Berlin!

Berlin   This is nice.

Adele   You're hurting.

Berlin   A chance to . . . touch.

Adele   You're not like this.

Berlin   We need to explore each other more . . .

Adele   Let me go now.

Berlin *forces her to the floor. He puts his hand over her mouth.*

Berlin   Where's there to go? At this time of night . . . We've got the evening to ourselves . . . a crisp autumn evening all to ourselves. A still night . . . not a sound. Shhh! can you hear? My voice is echoing in the forest . . .

16   Solidarity

Fret *and* **Sava** *in the station waiting room.* **Sava** *is nursing his wounds. Meanwhile, in the street near the Calypso* **Morocco** *staggers and falls, brutally beaten.*

Sava   What are you thinking about?

Fret   What's happening to things, Sava?

Sava   Is it the station?

Fret   Not just the station, not just us but . . . everywhere
I look . . . It feels like things are crumbling . . . I've lived in this
town all my life. Since I was a boy I've never been anywhere
else. I've seen buildings go up and come down, I've seen street
names change . . . it's formed around me like geology. And
now it's wearing away. It's eroding in the wind. Losing tiny
particles of substance every day, getting smaller,
breaking up.

Sava   You're upset. Berlin's upset you. Believe me, I've seen
it before.

Fret   I didn't know what to say to him. I just . . . stood.

Sava   When there's nothing to say, silence is at least a
dignified response.

Fret   But I let him say those things about this town. I just
stood. Let it happen.

Sava   If people want to know the truth about this town they
only need to come here. They'll soon see it's not the way
Berlin wants it. People only need to turn up.

Fret   They won't be able to find it. They'll just see a
blur from the train. Express trains going so fast they can't
even make out the station name as they pass. That's all
that'll be left of us. The home you thought you had, the
place you thought you came from, the person you thought
you were . . . whoosh! Whooosh! Gone past. Dust on the
breeze. By the time they think to turn up it'll already be
gone.

Katia *arrives and sees* **Morocco**. *He is regaining consciousness
painfully.* **Katia** *is smoking.*

Katia   I ran away. I hid. If you were wondering.

Morocco   I know.

Katia   I'm sorry.

Morocco   What for?

Katia   For you. Sorry you got hit.

Morocco   Thank you.

Katia   I'm not sorry I ran away.

Morocco   Don't be.

Katia   I would have brought help but . . . you know.

Morocco   I know.

Katia   I don't like to deal with the police. I feel uncomfortable with uniforms of any kind, the police especially.

Morocco   Don't explain.

Katia   There was no point in me staying. I wouldn't have been any use.

Morocco   None.

Katia   They'd have only got more excited. If I'd stayed. I'd have been a prize of some kind . . . they think that way. It happens, I've seen it. Once they've tasted blood . . . you know . . . sharks, they're like sharks.

Morocco   You did the right thing. I'm glad you're safe.

Katia's *hardness crumbles slightly. She crouches beside him.*

Katia   Your nose . . . it's bleeding . . . I wouldn't have been any use. My fists are like sponges. I can't fight.

Morocco   Did you see? Did you see who they were?

Katia   I heard. I couldn't see.

Morocco   What did you hear?

Katia   Thumping. A lot of thumps.

Morocco (*a moment of utterly impotent rage*)   I'll kill the fucking little shits, I'll fucking –

Katia I didn't see who they were. I'm sorry. It seemed more important to hide.

Morocco Just local boys . . . could have been any of them . . . probably all of them. I didn't see. There were a few.

Katia You were lucky . . . by the looks of it. You got away lightly.

Morocco At least they didn't have knives.

Katia Every cloud has a silver lining.

Morocco You've still got the papers? The passports?

Katia I made sure.

Morocco I must have looked a fucking prick. Trousers down in the shit.

Katia Don't think about it.

Morocco They got their money's worth out of me. I gave them a good show.

Katia Try and forget it.

Morocco I remember seeing the rings on his fist . . . I remember just the smallest part of a second having time to think. Fuck. Oh fuck.

Katia Shhh.

Morocco In the moment between turning round and his fist connecting with my nose. I had time to think . . . fuck, there's four of them . . . I thought fuck, my trousers are round my ankles . . . and I thought fuck he's wearing rings.

Katia I'm sorry I ran away.

Morocco After that my recollection's a bit hazy . . . you understand.

Katia I can imagine. I don't need the details.

Morocco No.

Katia I know we're supposed to stick together people like us. I know it's expected.

Morocco   I didn't expect it.

Katia   It's just . . . I've found solidarity often just means more people get hurt and what's the point of that?

Morocco   I was the unlucky one this time. Next time it could be you . . . then I'd run away.

Katia   Exactly. Best take your turn and hope for the best. It's not very life affirming, is it?

Morocco   Sometimes life's not very life affirming.

Katia   No. Your nose . . . poor Morocco.

Morocco (*winces*)   Please. I'm fine. I think it would be best if we got off the streets.

Katia   If you still want to fuck. You did pay after all. I've got my passports . . . we still have a deal?

Morocco   I don't feel like it.

Katia   No I suppose not.

Morocco   The day after tomorrow. A bus comes through in the afternoon. Adele'll know the time.

Katia   You should get home. It's late. It's after midnight. You should have a wash . . . you don't want infections . . .

Morocco   I will.

Katia   I'm sorry I ran away.

Morocco   I know. I'd have done the same. In your shoes I'd have done the same.

Express train passing.

17   Foreigners out

The bus stop. **Horse**'s *earlier writing of 'foreigners out' remains. It's very cold.* **Katia**, **Adele** *and* **Sava** *are waiting for a bus. It's dark and quiet. Although there is obviously a great deal of emotion none is*

shown or expressed except in **Katia**'s *holding of her father's hand.*
Sava's *face shows the signs of his recent beating. After some moments a*
bus arrives.

18 Blame

Fret *is sitting in a comfortable chair.* **Sava** *stands nearby.*

Sava   She went.

Fret   They go eventually. It's inevitable.

Sava   You're right. It's not a comfort though, is it? That it's
inevitable?

Fret   No.

Sava   I think she considers me to blame.

Fret   For what?

Sava   . . .
Most of it.
She blames me for protesting, here, she says we drew
unnecessary attention to ourselves.
Brought down the fists upon myself, she thinks.
Probably right.
Still, that's not what hurts.

Fret   The face?

Sava   The face? My face?

Fret   Does it hurt?

Sava   No, it's numb. I'm a little drunk so it's numb. It's not
my face that hurts but that she blames me for the other
thing.

Fret   What other thing?

Sava   The past.

Fret   You're not responsible.

Sava   The war, you know.

Fret   It's not your fault, surely.

Sava   You know they . . . She was . . . assaulted. She was – a
lot of people were assaulted – but . . . I think she was – she
never says but I think – she blames me for making her stay.
Making her stay so that what happened to her could happen
to her. I thought it was our duty as citizens not to desert our
homes. As a result . . .

Fret   You can't have known.

Sava   Perhaps I did know. Looking back, I think I probably
did. But I'm, by nature, a person who stays. I'm not sorry. I'm
sorry she blames me but I'm not sorry that we stayed. By
staying I think we brought a sliver of dignity, a sliver of
civilization to an otherwise damned place. We can't leave
places to the wolves. Still, dignity always costs something. I
think she blames me.

Fret   You decided not to go with her this time?

Sava   I've found myself here. In a station. A station is a
place to finish a journey as well a place to start one.

Fret   I'm glad you made that decision.

19   Wolves

Berlin *and* **Horse**. **Fret** *and* **Sava** *in the station.*

Berlin   The radio said it was the coldest October night for a
decade and a half. There wasn't a cloud, just the dark and the
stars. Horse kept saying he wished he'd brought a hat. He
should have brought a hat. And he kept rubbing his ears . . .
anyway we'd soon be warm enough – Did you bring the
vodka?

Horse   Of course I did.

Berlin   Of course he had. Of course he'd brought the
vodka. It was the coldest October night for a decade and a

half and the vodka left a beautiful burn around the heart. A burn that spread out across the chest, oiling the veins and arteries, loosening muscles, heating nerve ends . . .

Horse Berlin, I've . . . (*Hiccup.*) shi . . . (*Hiccup.*)

Berlin Shhh.

Horse I've got the hiccups.

Berlin Shh.

Horse I've got the fucking hiccups. (*Laughing.*)

Berlin Hold your breath.

Horse *draws in breath.*

Berlin Put your head between your legs.

Horse *puts his head between his legs.*

Berlin One two three . . .

Although not asleep, **Fret** *and* **Sava** *have been in a waking dream.*

Fret Shhh! Did you hear something?

Sava Hmmm?

Fret Shhh.
. . .
Do you hear?
A giggling . . . a giggling

Sava I heard something . . . a rustling . . . I'm not sure I'd call it a giggling though.

Fret I'd swear – maybe not a giggle but something like a giggle.

Sava You were dreaming. You just heard voices in your dream.

Fret You're probably right. I've been soaking in the vodka too long. What time's it?

Sava (*looking at station clock*) It's late. Or early . . . depending how you look at it.

Fret (*looking at station clock*)   I'd say it was late. I must have drifted off. It's cold.

Sava   Bitter.

Fret   We should go inside. I've made you up a bed in the office.

Sava   A little longer. It's a beautiful night. We'll finish the bottle.

Horse *stands, exhales.*

Berlin   Fifty. And again.

Horse *takes in a deep breath, holds it and bends double again.*

Fret   Wait a minute. I heard it again.
. . .
I heard voices.
I'm sure of it.

Sava   Sure . . . ?

Fret   No.

Horse *lets out a huge breath.*

Fret   What was that?

Berlin   Come on . . . Hurry up.

Horse   I can hear voices inside.

Berlin   Give me the matches. It's fucking freezing, my hands are shaking, look. (*His hands are shivering.*) I am fucking freezing, Jesus Christ, give us a nip.

Horse   Shut up. Shut up, they'll hear us.

Berlin   Christ, I can't light the frigging match. I can't light the match. My hands are jelly. Give us a nip. Give us a fucking nip. (*He takes a swig of vodka.*)

Fret   Probably wolves.

Sava   Wolves?

Fret   There's a pack in the forest. They crossed the forest when the border came down.

Sava   They came back to the hills near our town after the war started. You could hear them howling in the suburbs. Horrible.

Fret   I used to hate it . . . being on my own. On nightshift. I don't like the dark.

Sava   Me neither.

Fret   I used to ask myself what I was afraid of. Who'd want to attack a stationmaster? I hadn't any money to rob.

Sava   So what were you afraid of?

Fret   That's just it. I could never pin it down. Animals. It might have been the forest, the dark or even the trains.

Sava   What's there to be scared of in a train?

Fret   You don't know what it's bringing you. You don't know what it's going to take away.

Berlin   It's lit. Throw it.

Horse   What?

Sava   I heard something that time.

They both listen.

Horse *lights a cloth and stick it into the top of a bottle.*

Berlin   Fucking throw it.

Horse   Wait a minute!

Berlin   What?

Fret   Come on, we'll go inside.

Sava   Too cold to be out here.

Fret   Yes. Too cold. Yes. It's probably nothing anyway.

Sava   Probably nothing at all.

Berlin   Come on!

Horse   Where?

Berlin   What?

Horse   Where? Throw it where?

Berlin   I don't care.

Horse   It's going to explode.

Berlin   I don't know where.

Horse   It's going to explode.

Berlin   Anywhere. In there.

Horse   But I heard voices.

Berlin   Fuck the voices. (*He takes the bottle from* **Horse**.)

Horse   Berlin!

Berlin   So I threw it.

Fret *is in the office.* **Sava** *on his way.*

Sava   It's just imagination, Fret. If there's one thing I learned in the yards about staying awake on a long night it's keep the old imagination under control. Don't let the old mind invent things to frighten itself. Don't conjure up demons. Don't talk to ghosts.

Berlin   There was just the smallest moment of total silence and we saw the little flame curve through the air . . . then the familiar sound; the pleasant, reassuring sound of bottle on concrete and the flame taking. We ran. We ran into the forest.

Horse   Oh Christ Jesus God cunt fuck.

Berlin   From the forest we stood and watched it go up. It seemed like seconds to me. Less than seconds. Like a bomb. There was no stopping it. On the news the fireman said the station was a tinderbox. He said it was criminal. Criminal that it could have been left in that condition. They didn't have a chance he said. No one stood a chance in that place. Criminal.

LOOK AT IT LOOK AT IT LOOK AT IT! . . . IT'S
BEAUTIFUL.

At first we just saw the light inside. Just an orange glow inside
and then some smoke. It was a clear night so we could see the
smoke rising. Even from that distance we could feel it warm.
AMAZING. (*He holds out the back of his hand.*)
I CAN FEEL IT. I CAN FEEL IT FROM HERE!
It was comforting. The heat. The light. The timbers cracking.
Like working the furnace. Like standing next to a brazier on
the night shift.

*The noise of a train is beginning slowly in the distance. However it is, at
least initially, imperceptible, growing during the rest of the speech.*

The express train passes . . . this time however the noise continues.

20   Europe

Adele and **Katia** *are in the toilets on an international train.* **Katia**
is sitting on the toilet. **Adele** *has opened the window and is looking
out.*

Katia   He'll be all right. Won't he? He'll register and – Fret
was good about things. Fret was a godsend. He likes company.
Dad needs company.

Adele   Where are we going to go to first?

Katia   It's your town. You know it, what it's like. Will he be
all right?

Adele   Let's go to Berlin . . . for the cabaret.

Katia   I said he should come with us but he's tired of
travelling.

Adele   Vienna. Vienna for the cakes.

Katia   And it's easier, when you're on your own to go
unnoticed. To look after yourself. To slip past guards . . . It's
best he stayed. He seemed happy. Did you think he was
happy?

Adele   Portugal. I never even thought of Portugal.

Katia   I feel responsible. He needs looking after.

Adele   Come and look . . . come and look out the window.

Katia   Are we out of the forest?

Adele   Not yet, do you know which way we're going?

Katia   West.

Adele   Which mountains are we in?

Katia   I don't know.

Adele   It doesn't matter. We're in mountains.

Katia   It was the right thing to leave. That's the main thing.
It was the right decision.

Adele   Paris . . . we'll go to Paris . . . for the romance . . .
(*Kisses* **Katia** *briefly.*) Milan . . . we'll go to Milan.

Katia   Maybe.

Adele   Or Prague.

Katia   Perhaps.
. . . Perhaps . . . if you think about it . . . I suppose we were
lucky to be blown into your station . . . perhaps it was just as
well.

Adele   Just as well? It was the best thing that ever happened.

Katia   I'm not sure I would go so far as to say that.

Berlin   The next day, after the fire, the government minister
came to see the ashes. He said they would stamp us out. He
said . . . these monsters aren't part of our nation. They don't
belong in our midst. He said we have to drive them out.
There's no place for them here. No place for them anywhere.

Adele   We'll go to Moscow . . .

Katia   We could go to Petersburg.

Berlin   The country has been sitting on a powderkeg for too long. A spark was bound to catch. He said he'd tighten up on immigration controls. After all . . . feelings were running high all over the continent.

Adele *kisses* **Katia**. **Katia** *finally kisses back. They begin to kiss sexually. Their hands exploring each other.*

Adele   To Venice.

Katia   To Rome.

Berlin   He said it was a tragedy. A terrible tragedy. And he said he was making a ministerial visit. The problems were being considered at the highest level.

Katia   To Rotterdam.

Adele   To Copenhagen.

Berlin   We were on the television. On the front of magazines. Me and Horse, we were discussed on the radio. Protest songs were written about us.

Adele   Sofia.

Katia   Budapest.

Berlin   They said the name of our town, politicians and sociologists all across the continent said its name.

Adele   Barcelona.

Katia   Marseilles.

Berlin   Until it wasn't a name any more but a condition, not a place but an effect.
But it was our town.

Adele   Athens.

Katia   Hamburg.

Berlin   For one day, for one week . . . maybe even for a month. Everyone knew the name of our town. And now they know. They know that even as they travel to some older . . .

Adele   Salzburg.

Berlin   Or more beautiful . . .

Katia   Sarajevo.

Berlin   Or more important place.

Adele   Just imagine.

Katia   Shh . . .

Berlin   They know that, in our own way, we're also Europe.

Lights down . . . the noise of the train continues for a few moments in the dark.

The Architect

For Mum, Dad and Mike

'The Smoke'

A little house among trees by the lake
From the roof smoke rises
Without it
How dreary would be
House, trees and lake.

Bertolt Brecht

The Architect was first performed at the Traverse Theatre, Edinburgh, on 23 February 1996. The cast was as follows:

Leo Black	Alexander Morton
Martin Black	Tom Smith
Sheena Mackie	Una McLean
Paulina Black	Morag Hood
Dorothy Black	Ashley Jensen
Joe	Eric Barlow
Billy	Paul Hickey

Directed by Philip Howard
Designed by Simon Vincenzi
Lighting by Chahine Yavroyan
Music by Reuben Taylor

Characters

Leo Black, *an architect, fifties.*
Paulina Black, *his wife, forties.*
Martin Black, *his son, twenties.*
Dorothy Black, *his daughter, twenties.*
Joe, *a lorry driver, forties.*
Billy, *a young man, twenties.*
Sheena Mackie, *a campaigner, fifties.*

Setting: A city. The present.

Act One

1

Darkness.
The long blast of a siren.
A moment of silence.
A series of explosions.
Large buildings falling to the ground.
A crowd applauding.

2

A summer afternoon.
A building site.

A small trestle table stands centre stage. On the table are architectural plans and blueprints. The papers are weighted down with stones to stop them blowing away. Two hard hats are on the table.

Martin *is looking casually at the blueprints.*
Leo *enters carrying an architectural model, it is bulky, he is struggling with it.* **Martin** *looks.*

Leo   Some professions, Martin, exist only or mainly, to provide particular people with a congenial way of earning their living. Publishing, for example, or radio, you mentioned radio. These people, these publishers and so on, they're interesting. I've met them sometimes. They're creative people. Their surroundings are, if you like, seductive. But in the end, these are people without effect in the world. Do you see what I'm saying. They have no . . . power to shape, no responsibility. Now, building, construction, engineering, architecture. These have effects. Here you have responsibility. Obviously you can dream, use your imagination, of course, but there's a purpose. You put your dreams on paper . . . blueprints, drawings.

The smallest line, the merest gesture of the pencil, can be the curve of a motorway flyover, or pull a tower up from the slums, or shape a square from a mess of alleys. That's what we do, Martin, we dream these structures and then.

Martin   It's flat.

Leo   Sorry?

Martin   This. Here. I thought you built. I thought you were a builder. This is flat.

Leo   This is the car park. It's supposed to be flat.

Martin   Oh.

Leo   To go back, we dream these structures, these buildings and –

Martin   You said there was going to be a tower. There's a tower on the model.

Leo   The buildings take shape, become solid.

Martin   There's no tower here.

Leo   People live in them, work in them . . .

Martin   There's some lumps.

Leo   We have an effect. You understand?

Martin *refers to the model.*

Martin   Nothing like that.

Leo   The tower's going to be over there. At the head of the docks. Where the fish market used to be. They're still digging foundations. But you can imagine.

Martin   Is this one of yours? The tower? Did you dream it?

Leo   A lot of people are involved on the project.

Martin   Did you think it up though? Your dream?

Leo   I'm part of the design team, obviously . . . so in that sense, yes. Everyone has their role, everyone has input.

Martin   What's your input?

Leo   Well, the car park's mine. My job on the team is access. So clearly . . . parking – which is important on a project like this . . . also security, the walls, if you like.

Martin   They're big.

Leo   Well spotted.

Martin   Thick.

Leo   Look around you, Martin – beyond the fencing, over there – what do you see?

Martin   Houses. Some people.

Leo   Houses, yes, but – look at the immediate environment – the surroundings.

Martin   . . .

Leo   Understand? This site's in the middle of no-man's-land. Look at it. Devastation. Someone in the planning department told me, this is officially third world status. Which means vandalism, burglars, and Christ knows whatever else. It's a prime example.
You dream up ideas, but you have to think, you have to see potential problems. Solve them. Before they happen – understand? I saw the problem – that . . . and this is the physical solution.

Martin   Big walls.

Leo   Metaphorically, yes, I suppose so.

Martin   How high?

Leo   Four metres, plus barbed wire . . .

Martin   The tower. How high?

Leo   Square footage?

Martin   How many floors?

Leo   Seventeen.

Martin   How high can you build something?

Leo   In what way do you mean high?

Martin   Up the way high? How high can a thing be built? Anything?

Leo   It's an interesting question.

Martin   Interesting.

Leo   Design, materials and nature are what you have to think about. A good design can take poor materials higher. Good materials can support a poor design. And then there's nature – wind, damp, heat, earthquakes, the imponderables. You overcompensate for nature . . .

Martin   How high then?

Leo   The base of the building would have to be wide . . . to support the height. Lifts are a problem, over a certain number of floors and you need separate lifts . . . then there's the human elements . . . vertigo. People do get vertigo. I suppose that counts as nature. Materials, design and nature . . . if one of these factors is out of harmony then, when you get beyond a certain point, the structure overbalances, things get dangerous. You can work it out. Theoretically, though, there's no limits.

Martin   Can you build a thing high enough that if you fell off you wouldn't hit the ground?

Leo   . . .

Martin   High enough so that if you fell, you'd fall into orbit?

Leo   This is offices, Martin. No one's going to fall out.

Martin   Could you though?

Leo   Is this a joke?

Martin   I'm only asking –

Leo   It feels like you're making a joke.

Martin   I'm not, honestly.

Leo   I thought you wanted to talk about work.

Martin   I was.

Leo   If you're bored.

Martin   I'm not bored . . . I was asking a question.

Leo   It sounded like a joke. I'm sorry.

Martin   Doesn't matter. Forget it.

Leo   Put this on.

Leo *gives* **Martin** *a hardhat.*

Martin   What for?

Leo   Safety. It's to protect your head.

Martin   From what?

Leo   Everyone on site has to wear a hard hat. It's
regulations.

Martin   But there's nothing above us. It's flat. Only lumps.

Leo   We're on site, Martin. Accidents happen. You'll wear a
hard hat.

Martin   I'm just saying –

Leo   What the hell is the problem with you?
There's no pain in wearing it.
It won't hurt your head.
I said to put it on.

Martin *puts the hat on.*

Martin   I look like one of the Village People.

Leo   What?

Martin   Doesn't matter.

Leo   You mutter, Martin, do you know that? You're a
mutterer. Under your breath. You speak behind your hand.
Do you notice yourself doing it?

Martin (*muttering*)   No.

Leo   If you've got something to say. Say it clearly. Make the point.

. . .

You have to think about your presentation.
Think about how you come across.

. . .

He offers **Martin** *a cigarette.*

Martin   I don't smoke.

Leo   Quite right too.

He tries to light his cigarette. He can't get the lighter to work.

Too windy.

He turns and cups his hand. The lighter still doesn't work.

Damn.

He lifts his jacket to use as a windbreak. Again he fails.

Damn.

Martin   I thought you'd given up.

Leo   Not yet.

Martin   Mum said she didn't let you smoke in the house any more.

Leo   We're not in the house.

Martin   Die if you want to.

Leo   You're muttering again. Stand here.

Martin *stands in front of* **Leo** *to block the wind.*

Martin   I said, 'Die if you want to.'

Leo   Closer.

Martin *stands closer.*

Martin   Man your age. Your job. You're probably due a stroke.

Leo Closer.

Martin *and* **Leo** *stand uncomfortably close. The cigarette is finally lit.* **Martin** *moves away.*

Leo So. What do you think?

Martin About what?

Leo The work. Does it appeal?

Martin ...?

Leo Are you interested or not?

Martin ...?

Leo Do you want the job?

Martin What job?

Leo What do you think I've been talking about?

Martin I don't know. Stuff.

Leo I wanted you to see the work.
I'm offering you a job, Martin.
You don't do anything . . . you're drifting . . . you don't – I've been thinking, for a while now, just the time hasn't been right, I've been considering the idea of setting up on my own. Small scale. Nothing big, not yet anyway. It's only an idea at the moment but this job's coming to an end and . . .
I want to get back to . . . a certain control. Understand?
This work, there's prestige but there's no control.

Martin Who builds the models?

Leo Never mind the model. Are you interested?

Martin You used to let me play with these, when you'd finished with them. I put toy soldiers in the buildings . . . I staged riots, assassinations and things, street to street fighting, car bombs and earthquakes.

Leo They're technical models. They're not toys.

Martin They're so delicate. So perfect. They look solid but you only have to nudge them and something breaks.

Leo   You could have damaged them.

Martin   The model's clean. Is that deliberate? When you make them? They don't look anything like real buildings. There's no dirt. No mess around them. Just white card, patches of green felt and pretend trees. They look like film buildings. They look as though the sun's always shining on them.

Leo   Do you want to work with me or not?
. . .
It would be a job.

Martin   Can I do the models?

Leo   You'd have to start at the bottom . . . but you'd be trained. I could start you off with –

Martin   I could be in charge of making the models look real. Cover the walls in graffiti or something . . . put little models of dossers under the bridges . . . Use my know-how. Could I do that?

Leo   Why don't we have a look at the foundations?

Martin   Whatever you say, boss.

Leo   You can see how the building takes shape.

Martin   Whatever you want, boss.

Sheena *has entered. She stands by the model. She is carrying some papers.*

Leo   I want to know what you want, Martin. I know what I want. I'm trying to help you.

Martin   Dad, there's –

Leo   I don't expect you to be interested, you know. You don't have to pretend – Obviously you're interested in other things. Whatever. I don't know. You don't tell me. If you told me, maybe I could get in touch with someone –

Martin   Foundations – fine. Dad – there's a woman –

Leo   You mentioned radio. Maybe I could ring someone.

Martin   Cheers. But –

Leo   I have some contacts. I just thought it was possible you'd be interested in working for me.

Martin   I said. I said I was interested.

Leo   Don't do me any favours.

Martin   All right. I'm not interested.

Leo   Well, what then? What exactly do you want?

Martin   Do you need a bicycle courier?

Sheena   Excuse me.

Leo   Sorry?

Martin   I tried to tell you.

Sheena   Mr Black?

Martin   She's been stood there waiting.

Sheena   Leo Black? Sorry to bother you. My name's Sheena Mackie. I haven't caught you at a bad time, have I?

Leo   No . . . I'm sorry. Are you supposed to be here?

Sheena   I'll only take a minute. I've got a taxi waiting.

Leo   Do you have a site pass?

Sheena   I didn't know I needed one?

Leo   No one's allowed on site without a pass . . . I'm sorry it's regulations.

Sheena   Well. I'm here now so maybe we could have a chat.

Leo   It's Saturday morning, Mrs . . .

Sheena   Mackie, it's actually Ms. As I say, I'll only be a minute, the thing is I've tried to get you at your office, but you always seem to be busy . . . I don't know if you remember the letter? I've put a copy in with the petition.

Leo   Petition? You've lost me.

Sheena   I'm the tenants' representative. From Eden Court.
We wrote to you about the flats weeks ago now.

Leo   What letter?
I haven't seen any –
Just a minute. Martin, could you get the phone from the car?

Sheena   I wouldn't normally bother you but things are
moving on. We need to keep things going. For the campaign.
Your wife said you'd be down here. I thought I'd take the
chance to catch you.

Leo   There's obviously been some –
Some kind of mix up.
I'm sure we can sort it out. The thing is . . . you need a site
pass. You understand we can't have people wandering round,
in case there's an accident. If you hold on, my son'll ring the
security people. Martin, could you give Mrs Mackie your hat.
While you're on site you need a hard hat. In case anything
falls on your head. For insurance . . .

Martin *gives her his hat.*

Leo *begins reading the folder of papers.*

Sheena   I feel like the Queen visiting the shipyards.

Martin   What about me?

Leo   What?

Martin   I don't have a hat now.

Leo   Just get the phone.

Sheena   I won't be a minute. The meter's running. Is that
your son?

Martin   Do you want me to answer?

Leo   He helps me.

Sheena   Are you a builder as well?

Leo   Architect.

Martin   Bicycle courier.

Sheena   Well. Pleased to meet you.

Martin   Martin.
Do you still want me to get the phone?

Leo   Yes.

Sheena   Like Dean Martin.

Martin   What?

Sheena   Before your time.

Martin   No.

Leo   I don't follow this, Mrs Mackie.
This petition you've got here.
This correspondence.
It's been sorted out. The council have spoken to me about the
Eden Court flats. I've talked to them about it. They're going
to refurbish them . . . I've sent designs . . . I don't see what
you're getting at.

Martin   Martin Sheen maybe.

Sheena   You didn't know?

Leo   No.

Sheena   I'm not sure how to say this.
The problem is . . . we . . .
I mean, us, the tenants . . . we don't want the flats refurbished.

Martin   Martin Luther King.

Bored, **Martin** *has begun to play with the model, piling buildings on
top of each other. Moving them around.*

Leo   But they need work. Some of those blocks haven't been
maintained for years.

Martin   Martina Navratilova.

Leo   I told the housing executive. They'll fall apart if work
isn't done on them soon. The surveyor's report was – Martin,
don't do that!

Martin   Just curious.

Leo   The problem's under control. The work's being done for you.

Sheena   We don't want the flats done up, Mr Black. We want them knocked down.

Leo   . . .

Sheena   We've got a petition. Signed by every resident. That copy's for you. There's a copy gone to the council, one to the paper and one to Prince Charles. He signed it.

Leo   Christ.

Sheena   Well, he's interested in that sort of thing, isn't he? Buildings. He's concerned. Not professionally but like an ordinary person. Isn't he?

Leo   He's not an architect. No.

Sheena   Mr Black, we just want houses. We've been in Eden Court, some of us, for twenty years. This isn't a new problem. We've tried but things have gone too far now. We're not interested in plastering over the cracks any more. We want to live in proper houses, decently built.

Leo   I see.

Sheena   It's nothing personal.

Leo   Of course.

Sheena   No offence.

Leo   None taken.

Sheena   You'll consider the petition then?

Leo   I don't really see how I can help you.

Sheena   You can give us your support.

Leo   To demolish my own buildings?

Sheena   Our flats.

Leo   My design.

Martin   You could bomb them.

Leo   I don't see why you need my signature.
I'd have thought there was plenty people who wanted to see the back of Eden Court.

Martin   From the sky. Planes.

Leo   People in this country don't like anything unless it's thatched.

Martin   Smart bombs.

Sheena   The council don't want to build a new estate. They say there isn't the money. It's cheaper to slap a bit of paint on and leave the place to fall apart. We could take them to court but something like this could take years. The only way we'll get what we want is if we embarrass the council. And if you say they need to be rebuilt they'll have to do something. They can hardly argue with the architect, can they?

Leo   Or Prince Charles.
. . .
You're very well organised, Mrs Mackie. This is . . . it's impressive.

Sheena   Thank you.

Leo   You've put a lot of work into it.

Sheena   We have.

Leo   There's obviously . . . a lot of strong feeling in what you say.

Sheena   Obviously.

Leo   But the feelings are misdirected, I'm afraid.
The Eden Court flats are good buildings.
Technically.

Martin   What's wrong with them?

Sheena   They're cold, the lifts don't work.

Leo   There's nothing wrong with the design.

Martin   Is that all?

Sheena   Most of the flats are infested with cockroaches.

Leo   There wasn't enough money spent on them at the time.

Martin   Get Rentokil.

Leo   But if the council are prepared to spend the money now I don't see the need for destruction.

Sheena   They're a new breed of cockroach. A new mutation. There's been a documentary.

Leo   If you look at my proposals –

Sheena   They can't be killed in the ordinary way.

Leo   I realise that, I understand there's a depth of emotion. Tower blocks do cause . . . passion. I know that. But if I could . . . persuade you about this . . . I don't think there needs to be . . .

Sheena   We're not asking you to say sorry or anything, Mr Black. We just want you to consider the petition. These signatures. That's the people that live in Eden Court.

Leo   But destruction.

Sheena   People get things wrong . . . that's fair enough.

Leo   These are understandable grievances but –

Sheena   You've got a chance to help fix it.

Leo   Individual problems like this can be solved.

Sheena   You've got a chance to make things right.

Leo   You can't just blow something up for no reason . . . You can't just destroy something that's perfectly sound.

Sheena   Look, Mr Black. The taxi's waiting. Now that we've met. Actually made contact. Maybe I could arrange an appointment. Talk to you once you've read everything.

Leo   I won't change my mind. I'm sorry.

Sheena   You know, it's funny to think it was you that built them.

Leo   Is it?

Sheena   Not you in particular. I just mean it's funny to think someone thought them up. You know, a person. You always feel as though they just happened. You're not insulted, are you?

Leo   I assure you –

Sheena   It's just . . . seeing you. Face to face, I mean. It's funny.
Well. I'll be in touch. (*To* **Martin**.) Nice to have met you.

Sheena *leaves.* **Martin** *considers the model. Now considerably rearranged.*

Leo   Jesus Christ.

Martin   Boom.

Leo   What?

Martin   Boom.

Lights down.

3

Later. A suburban garden. **Dorothy** *is sitting on a deckchair wearing a short summer dress and sunglasses. A radio is playing quietly beside her. On a table in the garden is a pile of delicate sandwiches and a jug of lemonade.* **Paulina** *is examining her plants. She is overdressed for the sun and wearing gardening gloves. She touches a plant.*

Paulina   Black. See? Half an inch of black poison on the stem. You should cover up. That's just what's hanging in the air. It's worse in the sunshine. Some sort of chemical reaction takes place with the sun, makes it worse, apparently. You should cover up. You'll burn. If that's what's hanging in the

air, imagine what's settling in your lungs and blood and
everything. Illnesses are up. Cancers are up. Sicknesses are up.
Dorothy? Are you listening to me. You'll burn alive under that
sun. Dorothy?

She smells a rose.

No scent. Proof. If proof were needed. The scent's been
poisoned out of them. They only look like flowers now. You
have to ask yourself what next. I saw a cyclist stop at the lights.
Imagine cycling, in this city, you could be dragged off and
beaten at any junction. He was wearing a surgeon's mask. It
was black. The gauze was black as tar. Like a swab soaked in
black blood. That's just what's in the air.

An aeroplane passes loudly overhead.

Dorothy.
Dorothy.
Dorothy!

The noise has quietened. The radio still plays.

You should cover up. You should cover up before whatever's
going to fall from the sky falls from the sky and gets on to your
skin. Your father'll be back soon.

. . .

She makes her way indoors.

. . . You won't tan, you know. You don't tan. You'll burn.
Look like a bad tomato. You should put some proper clothes
on.

Paulina *exits. The radio continues to play.* **Dorothy** *hitches her skirt
up her legs a little and rubs oil into them. She relaxes back in the
deckchair. After some moments* **Leo** *enters. He is hot. He walks in front
of* **Dorothy** *towards the house. He can't help but look at his daughter.
He stands by the sandwich table and agonisingly stares, looks away,
stares.*

Leo   Sandwiches.

Dorothy   Dad.

She pulls her skirt down.

Leo   They look . . . delicious.

Dorothy   Have one. They're for you.

Leo   I'll just . . .

Leo *takes a sandwich. He leaves.* **Martin** *has been watching. He waits till* **Leo** *is indoors. He goes over to the table and picks up a sandwich. He stares at* **Dorothy**. *He goes over to her and lifts her skirt.*

Martin   Nice cunt.

Dorothy *stops him.*

Dorothy   Don't.

Martin   Shame you're wearing pants.

Dorothy   Martin.

Martin   You don't think of your sister having a cunt, do you? Barbie-smooth, you imagine. Surprising.

Dorothy   Stop it.

Martin   Nice though. If that's what you like. Let him have a good look, did you?

Dorothy   He wasn't looking.

Martin   I just saw him.

Dorothy   Leave it, Martin.

Martin   It's understandable I suppose, at his age, no harm in a look.

Dorothy   Don't say that.

Martin   I can see the attraction. You sat there. So secretarial. So available.

Dorothy   What does that mean?

Martin   Does he do it at work? When you take dictation?

Dorothy   You've got a warped mind.

Martin   To think I sprang from his loins. Made of the same stuff. The scientists are baffled.

Dorothy   Please.

Martin (*taking another sandwich*)   Did you make these?

Dorothy   Yes.

Martin   I'm going to be a chef. I've been thinking about it. In France. I'll get taught. It's an admired art in France you know. Cuisine. Means kitchen and cooking. Same word. I think I might be a bastard.

Dorothy   You are.

Martin   No, really. An actual bastard. I think mum fucked someone else. I'm not like him, am I? Do you think I'm like him?

Dorothy   Yes.

Martin   No, I'm not. I'm like mum.

Dorothy   Why do you have to say such horrible things about him?
Why do you have to attack him?

Martin   I'm not attacking him.

Dorothy   You are. He thinks you avoid him.

Martin   I do.

Dorothy   He notices. He gets hurt. He wants this to work.

Martin   Dorothy, I came home because I ran out of money. No other reason.
A business arrangement.
. . .
Does that shock you?

Dorothy   If you just try, Martin.

Martin   It shocks me.

Leo *enters. He is carrying a deckchair and a whisky.*

Leo   Thought I'd take the sun.
Catch the last of it.
Lovely sandwiches.

Martin   I made them.

Leo   Did you?

Dorothy   I made them.

Leo   Still . . .

Martin   Have one.

Leo   No. I'm . . . not for me.

Martin   You said they were lovely.

Leo   Yes, they are. I mean. I meant they look lovely. Well done.

Martin   I'm thinking of setting up a sandwich bar.

Dorothy   Martin.

Martin   These are a sort of trial run. A place in the West End. Don't you think?

Dorothy   He's joking.

Martin   Sandwiches for offices, for people just passing by, someone's shopping, they're a bit peckish, they might fancy a sandwich. A BLT . . .

Dorothy   I made them.

Martin   B for bacon, L for lettuce and T for tomato. It's American.

Dorothy   He knows that.

Martin   The classic sandwich. Go on. Try one.

Leo   No. Thank you.

Martin   It's a good idea though, isn't it? Gap in the market.

Leo   It's not a good idea, Martin, it's rubbish.
Can we please stop talking about this? It's a perfect afternoon.

I don't want to argue on a perfect afternoon.

Martin   Who's arguing? What's the argument?

Dorothy   Stop it.

Leo   Why don't we just . . . enjoy the sun together? Martin, get yourself a chair, why don't you have a drink?

Leo *strips to the waist and settles into the deckchair. He closes his eyes.*
Dorothy *clutches herself suddenly, as though a wave of nausea has passed over her.*

Martin   Don't.
Don't do that.
It doesn't make any difference when you do that.
You always do that.
It's your oldest trick.

Leo*'s eyes are open although neither* **Dorothy** *nor* **Martin** *notice.*

Dorothy   I'm not . . . doing. I just –

Martin   I said it didn't make any difference.

Dorothy   Martin.

She reaches for him as she recovers. She tries to steady herself

Martin   Look at you.

Martin *leaves.*

Leo   Are you all right?

Dorothy   What?
. . .
Oh. Me? Fine. Yes. Just a bit . . . You know. Indigestion.
That's all.

Leo   I shouldn't have shouted at him, I just get, when he babbles like that I get . . .
I offered him the job, you know.

Dorothy   He told me.

Leo   I think he's interested.

Dorothy   We were talking about it just now.

Leo   What did he say?

Dorothy   He said he thought it was good . . . a good idea.

Leo   He likes the idea?

Dorothy   He said he thought it was, an interesting business arrangement.

Leo   He would be good at it, you know, he doesn't think so but he could do it . . . He only needs to get to grips with himself. He's still drifting but if I can . . . now that he's come home if we can bring him in . . . give him some solidity. He said he used to play with the models. When he was little. I'd forgotten that.

Dorothy   We could all work together.

Leo   No more big projects. That's what I said to him. I'm tired of big projects . . . they run away from you. We'll stay small . . . keep everything under control.
Do you enjoy working for me, Dorothy?

Dorothy   What do you mean?

Leo   Do you like it?

Dorothy   I love it. I mean. It's fine. It's good.

Leo   You do the mail, don't you?

Dorothy   Mostly. Why?

Leo   And my calls. Do you answer the phone usually or does Sylvia?

Dorothy   Have I done something wrong?

Leo   I'm just asking.

Dorothy   If there's a mistake I'll –

Leo   There's no mistake.
I was just asking . . . just thinking.

Dorothy   Tell me.

Leo   I don't know what I'd do without you. That's all.
I was just thinking.
I don't know what I'd do without you.

Lights down.

4

Darkness. The quiet dripping sound of a gents public toilet. **Martin** *stands at a urinal with an empty Jenners' bag next to him . . .*

5

The roar of motorway traffic. **Dorothy** *standing beside a motorway at night. Her thumb out for a lift. Cars and lorries thunder past.*

6

Leo *and* **Paulina** *in their bedroom.* **Paulina** *looking in the mirror.*

Leo   He said he was interested. He seems . . . when he talks
sense . . . I think we're making progress . . . Paulina?

Paulina   Hmm?

Leo   You've been sitting there for half an hour.

Paulina   I'm looking at my face.
It's changed.

Leo   It doesn't change when you look at it. It changes when
you look away. Get dressed. We need to go.

Paulina   Leo. I don't want to go.

Leo   What?

Paulina   I never said I wanted to go.

Leo   I've bought tickets. There's people expecting us.

Paulina   I've heard it's terrible.
Makes no sense apparently.
Apparently it's the product of a diseased imagination.
I don't want to wallow in it.

Leo   We sponsored it.
It's supposed to be important.
It's a state of the nation play.

Paulina   I don't like tragedy.

Leo   It's farce.

Paulina   You go. If you want to go.

Leo   It's colleagues and wives. It's a colleagues and wives
thing. I can't go alone.

Paulina   Stay then.

Leo   What do you want me to do? Do you want me to
stay?

Paulina   Do you notice anything about the bedroom,
Leo?

Leo   I'll stay if you want me to stay.

Paulina   A bed. Walls. Bedside table. Perfume. Face cream.
Can you smell anything?

Leo   I can't say I noticed.

Paulina   No. You don't notice it until you notice it. Then
you can't get rid of it.

Leo   I'll stay. I'll ring them and say you're ill.

7

The side of a motorway. The noise of traffic. **Dorothy** *hitching. A lorry
pulls up. Its headlights flood the stage. Blinding.* **Dorothy** *gets into the
lorry.*

8

The sound of drip ping water. The inside of a public toilet. **Martin** *is still standing at the urinal.* **Billy** *enters. He stands near* **Martin** *at the urinal. They move together. Suddenly* **Billy** *kneels.* **Martin** *holds his head.*

9

Dorothy *and* **Joe** *in the cab of* **Joe**'s *lorry.*

Dorothy   Sometimes I want to run at the side of a house.
I get the feeling.
A red-bricked gable end.
Just turn and run at it straight. Full speed, as though it
wasn't there. Smack it and feel the bricks cut me.
Feel my skull smack.
Slide down half conscious.
Pick myself up and do it again.

Joe   Any particular house?

Dorothy   Mine. Anyone's. It doesn't matter so long as it's
made of bricks. I don't even need to be near a house to get the
feeling. I could be anywhere. At a party, in the office, in a field
and suddenly I want to smash myself against an outside wall.

Joe   I get feelings like that sometimes.

Dorothy   Really?

Joe   All the time. In the lorry, on the motorway, now even.
I could just yank the steering wheel and twist off the road.
Plough into a bus full of schoolchildren and not stop.

He turns his hand on the steering wheel.

Just that.

He repeats the movement.

That's all it would take.
It's quite common to feel that, among lorry drivers.

Dorothy   Something stops you though?

Joe   Not much. The skin of the milk. Not much more than that. There was a lorry driver once. It was famous. He was driving his lorry across the Sahara Desert and he crashed . . . right into a tree.

Dorothy   I thought there weren't any trees in the Sahara Desert.

Joe   Only one. That's the point of the story. He crashes into the most isolated tree in the world. Nothing but emptiness and sand for thousands of miles in any direction and there's this tree and he hits it. Killed himself. Killed the tree. People said it was insanity or coincidence or fate but I can understand it. In the middle of the desert you see a tree, one tree and . . .

He repeats the movement.

. . . you drive at it.
Of course you do.

Dorothy   You shouldn't be allowed on the road.

Joe   All drivers get it. Coach drivers particularly. You wouldn't become a coach driver unless you were fascinated by death. It's all they talk about. Still. I don't want to worry you. Touch wood.

He touches **Dorothy**'s *leg, momentarily.*

How far are you going?

Dorothy   As far as you're going. Somewhere far away. As far away as possible.

Joe   Hull. And back.

Dorothy   Hull then.

10

The gents toilet. In a cubicle. **Billy** *is standing inside the Jenners' bag, his face turned against the wall.* **Martin** *is behind him with his hands between his legs.* **Billy** *turns round to kiss* **Martin**.

Martin   No.

Billy   Go on.

Martin   No.

Martin *almost pushes* Billy *away.*

11

Leo *eating.* **Paulina** *watching. Silence.*

Leo   This is nice.

Paulina   Do you think so?

Leo   Really.
Good.
Home cooking.

Paulina   I bought it.

Leo   Shame the kids . . .
Seems silly to call them kids . . .
Doesn't seem the right word, does it?
Shame they couldn't eat with us.
We should eat together more. As a family.
If I'd known we . . . I'd have asked . . .

Paulina   They're out. Didn't say where.

Leo   A family dinner. Now Martin's home. Everyone round the table. Do the washing up together . . . like we used to.

Paulina   Shut your mouth, Leo.

Leo   What?

Paulina   When you're eating. Shut your mouth.

Leo   Sorry.

Paulina   You always do it.
Have you noticed that?
You don't think I need to see what's in your mouth. I cooked it. I don't need a display.

Leo   It's delicious. Very well made. It should be on display.
Why don't you have some wine?

Paulina   No.

Leo *pours himself a glass.*

Leo   You remember Eden Court? Paulina?
The housing estate I did . . . for the council . . .
'71 I think, feels like yesterday of course,
Martin was just born.
A woman came to me today.
She wants it blown up.

Paulina   Are you having an affair?

Leo   . . .
I'm sorry?

Paulina   Have you had one? Recently?

Leo   What makes you think . . .

Paulina   I'm asking.

Leo   No. No. I haven't, Paulina. No.
. . .
I'm not having an affair.

Paulina   You wouldn't tell me if you were.

Leo   Is there some kind of problem here, you don't believe
me?

Paulina   You were chatting. You usually chat to me when
you feel guilty about something.

Leo   For God's sake. I was talking about work.

Paulina   I don't know how you can drink that.

Leo   I said they want to demolish Eden Court.

Paulina   They tread on them. The grapes.

Leo   A thing I built. They want to destroy it.

Paulina   There's probably sweat in it.

Leo   I thought you'd want to know. That's all.

Paulina   Foot diseases and whatever else.

Leo   It's traditional. Traditionally that's how they make wine.

Paulina   It turns my stomach.

Leo   It's a typical attitude, of course. Blame the architect. People are poor. Blame the architect. Place is a slum, blame the architect. They fill a place with pigs and then complain it's turned into a pigsty.

Paulina   They probably urinate, the treaders, for revenge.

Leo   What?

Paulina   Revenge. They probably laugh as it runs down their legs.

Leo   I don't think so.

Paulina   You don't know what goes on in a person's mind.

Leo   It's good wine.

Paulina   All sorts of thoughts.

Leo   I thought you liked claret.

Paulina   Shut your mouth, Leo, you're doing it again.

Leo   I never understand the point of table manners you know. Fork this side, fork that side. It's all class. There's no beauty in it. No truth. Do you know, in some countries, if you're enjoying a meal, it's considered polite to belch. When I was in Saudi –

Paulina   If you want to belch go into the garden.

Leo   I don't want to belch, I'm just saying –

Paulina   Make your noises there.

Leo   I'm making a point. Table manners aren't –

Paulina   Excuse me.

Paulina *gets up and leaves.*

Leo   Paulina!
Paulina.
. . .

He pours another glass. Lights a cigarette.

12

Billy *and* **Martin** *in the streets.* **Billy** *walks behind* **Martin**.
Martin *is trying to shake him off.*

Billy   Mister. Oi. Mister. Wait.

Martin   . . .

Billy *catches up with him.*

Billy   Billy.

Martin   What d'you want?

Billy   What's your name?

Martin   None of your fucking business.

Billy   Just asking.

Martin   If I'd wanted you to know my name I'd tell you it.
Wouldn't I?

Billy   I know but –

Martin   So stop following me.

Billy   I've never seen you there before.
You're new.
Usually old blokes.

Martin *begins to move off.* **Billy** *follows him.*

Billy   Married . . . pot bellies and smelly dicks.
You're not married, are you . . .

Martin   I told you to fucking stop.

Billy *points to a shop window. In the shop window is a green jacket on a stand.*

Billy   Have you seen this jacket.

Martin   You keep talking to me.

Billy   It's like that jacket. You know, the one John Wayne wore in *The Quiet Man*.

Martin   Stop it.

Billy   You'd suit green, you'd look good in it.

Martin   I'm going to walk away. If you follow me I'm going to run. If you keep following me I'm going to punch you.

Billy   D'you promise?

Martin   I'll hit your face and I'll keep hitting it until you leave me alone. You don't want that, do you?

Billy   Are you rich? You look quite rich. Are you?

Martin   . . .

Billy   Your accent. You could probably buy that jacket. As a present to yourself.

Martin   I warned you . . .

Martin *approaches* **Billy** *as if about to hit him.* **Billy** *suddenly turns and punches through the glass of the shop window.*

13

Leo *answers phone.* **Paulina** *enters.*

Leo   No comment.
No comment.
I'm sorry.
I've told you no comment.
The buildings are structurally sound.
That's all I'm prepared to say at the moment.
No comment.

Thank you.
Goodbye.
Fucking idiot.

. . .

Newspaper.
You should eat something.

Paulina No.

Leo You're making yourself ill.

Paulina Just the thought of it. I can't.

Leo It's a chicken, Paulina, just chicken.

Paulina I saw a programme about it.

Leo Perfectly good food.

Paulina Probably riddled with disease.

Leo It looks fine to me. You cooked it.

Paulina If you had an affair you wouldn't tell me, would you?

Leo *puts some food on a plate and pushes it towards her.*

Paulina No.

Leo You're not turning vegetarian on me, are you?

Paulina Maybe. Maybe I'll stop eating altogether.

Leo I'm not having an affair, Paulina. Now eat something.

Paulina Fruit. I'll be fruitarian.

Leo Jesus.

Paulina I couldn't plan for it. If you had an affair. I wouldn't know until it had happened.

Leo It won't happen.

Paulina You'd disguise your guilt by paying me more attention.

Leo Don't be stupid.

Paulina   You could infect me. I wouldn't know. I couldn't plan for it.

Leo   Christ, Paulina, you're like a needle picking at a splinter. Jab jab jab. We're having dinner. I don't need this kind of . . . this . . . whatever it is you're trying to prove. Can't you just . . . Make small talk, be normal, eat the chicken, for God's sake.

Paulina   The thought of bird flesh. Rotting inside me.

Leo   Why did you cook it then?
Why did you cook the fucking thing if you didn't want to eat it?

Paulina   Habit, probably.
. . .
I'm sorry.

Pause. **Paulina**, *still, quietly, begins to weep.* **Leo** *goes to her, stands behind her and holds her.*

Leo   Is something wrong? Did I say something? Paulina, what's the matter?

Paulina   Pesticides on fruit.

Leo   Paulina.

Paulina   The rain rains on it. Washes the chemicals off.

Leo   Love.

Paulina   And then the rain's dirty. Full of poison.

Leo *tries to kiss her neck.*

Leo   Please don't cry.

Paulina   Don't leave me, Leo.
Don't go away.

Leo   I'm not going anywhere.

Paulina   They've gone. Don't you go too.

14

A Country Kitchen motorway service station. **Dorothy** *and* **Joe** *are sitting at a table. Their chairs are fixed to the floor. The light is sterile. It is dark outside.* **Joe** *is drinking tea from a jumbo-sized paper cup.* **Dorothy** *has been sleeping.*

Dorothy   What time is it?

Joe   Late. Nearly home. I bought you a tea.

Dorothy   Thank you.

Joe (*sings*)   It's four in the morning and once more the dawning . . .
. . .
Don't you want it?

Dorothy   No. How close are we?

Joe   An hour or so.
It'll get cold. You should drink it.
A nice hot cup of tea.
Do you good. Rinse out the insides.

Dorothy   I don't like tea.

Joe   Everyone likes tea. Except snobs.
You're not a coffee drinker, are you?

Dorothy   I just feel a bit . . .
You know . . . a bit.

Joe   I thought you might be thirsty, that's all.

Dorothy *clutches herself. A wave of nausea passes over her.*

Joe   Are you all right?

Dorothy   Yes.

Joe   You don't seem it.

Dorothy   I'm fine. It's finished now.

Joe   Moaning and groaning.

Dorothy   Honestly. I know what it is. It's gone now.
Honestly.

Joe   Are you sure you don't want some tea?

Dorothy   No.

Joe   It's still warm. They gave me a jumbo cup.
They know me here. I'm a regular.
I always stop and I always have a jumbo.
I don't even have to ask.
The girls just know.
Do your parents know where you are?

Dorothy   No.

Joe   They must be worried.

Dorothy   No.

Joe   I'm sorry. I don't mean to pry. Only I get runaways.
Hitching. You feel responsible.

Dorothy   I just needed to get away. I'm not . . . It's just
something I do from time to time. No one worries.

Joe   If your father got hold of me he'd go mad. Wouldn't he?
If he could see us now?

Dorothy   He won't notice.

Joe   You've been away all night.

Dorothy   I'll be back in the morning.
Where are we now?

Joe   Junction 17.

Dorothy   What are we carrying?

Joe   Barbed wire. Sheet metal. Fences. Security gear.

Dorothy   Are we nearly there?

Joe   If you look out that window you can see the lights of the
skyscrapers, the tallest ones. See . . . that's forty miles away.
Forty miles. Amazing. Would he go mad? Your father?

Dorothy What's in between?

Joe What?

Dorothy Here and there.

Joe Road.

Dorothy There must be more than just road.

Joe Well. Road and . . .
Obviously there's towns.

Dorothy Which ones?

Joe Small ones. You know. More suburbs in fact. Suburbs you'd call them.
. . .
And fields I suppose.

Dorothy What do they grow?

Joe Cows I think. Mainly. It's cows you see anyway.

Dorothy *wipes her face with a napkin. She examines the napkin.*

Dorothy How long was I asleep?

Joe Most of the way. You just curled up on the seat.

Dorothy I'm sorry.

Joe Why?

Dorothy I didn't chat. I slept.

Joe I drive a truck. I'm used to my own company.
I wouldn't say I enjoy it but I tolerate it.
I'm like an old married couple. I tolerate myself.

Dorothy It was warm. You had the heater on. I couldn't keep my eyes open. I always sleep best in trucks.

Joe Did you dream?

Dorothy No dreams.

Joe You looked peaceful. Nice.

Dorothy   I'm sorry I slept. It wasn't what you wanted.

Joe   I enjoyed your presence. That was company enough. As a matter of fact it's nice to have a girl beside you as you drive. Do your parents know where you go? When you're on these trips?

Dorothy   They never ask.

Joe   With a boyfriend?

Dorothy   Probably.

Joe   Don't they want to meet him? Talk to him?

Dorothy   We don't have that in our family.

Joe   What?

Dorothy   Asking. Telling.

Joe   Still.

Dorothy   What do you mean nice?

Joe   . . .

Dorothy   Nice to have a girl.

Joe   I didn't mean to offend you. Any man would . . . would feel . . .

Dorothy   What?

Joe   It doesn't matter. I shouldn't have said.

Dorothy   Go on.

Joe   Just having a girl near you. Your skin on the seat. Your breathing. That's all.

Dorothy   Tell me.

Joe   You know.

Dorothy   Say.

Joe   Any man would. A girl.

Dorothy   I turned you on?

Joe   No.
Yes.
No. Not 'turned on'. That's not the right words.

Dorothy   What then.

Joe   Moved. I was moved.

Dorothy   In what way?

Joe   Powerfully.

Dorothy   Powerfully in what way?

Joe   This is stupid. Just forget I said anything.

Dorothy   I want to know.

Joe   It's a mixture of things . . . a man's feelings . . . they . . .
you become sort of . . . full of . . . wanting.

Dorothy   Wanting.

Joe   Please don't take offence.

Dorothy   I won't.

Joe   You want to . . . you know . . . touch her. Hold her
breasts in your . . . see her . . . you know.

Dorothy   Oh.

Joe   But then I felt something different.

Dorothy   What?

Joe   Sadness. I felt sad for you.

Dorothy   And . . .

Joe   Then I felt sad for me.

Dorothy   And.

Joe   Then I felt sad for us. For everybody.
Funny, isn't it?
. . .
I wanted to hold you.

Dorothy   Why?

Joe   I wanted to protect you. From men like me.

Dorothy   Is that all?

Joe   You're not revolted?

Dorothy   No.

Joe   You don't mind me saying things like this?

Dorothy   It's what I want.

Joe   My wife would never let me say things like this to her.

Dorothy   You could tell her.

Joe   You don't want your wife to know you have these thoughts. This. Me. Here. You. My heart thumping like this. A young woman. I couldn't stand it if she knew these things about me. Looking at girls. Looking at you. I mean. I love my wife.

Dorothy   Do you?

Joe   Not love exactly. Care. No. It's hard to know the word. There's a connection between a man and his wife. You can't break it. Sometimes I think she knows what's disgusting about me. You think she can read your mind. Horrible. But you never say anything. You just couldn't.

. . .

We should stop. Talking about this stuff.

Dorothy   We can stop if you want to. Do you want to?

Joe   No. It's all right.

. . .

Ask more.

Dorothy   Do you look at your wife? When she's asleep?

Joe   I used to but . . . your wife . . . it would be like looking at your mother.

Dorothy   Did you do anything else? Apart from look at me?

Joe   No.

Not really.

Dorothy Say.

Joe I didn't do anything.

Dorothy You said . . .

Joe I tried to touch you. I reached out my hand to . . .
Lift your . . .
But I didn't. I could feel you breathing on my fingertips.
Common decency to stop. Or fear. Skin of the milk. I wanted
to. Nearly fainted from it.
Why do you want to know all this?

Dorothy Why do you want to tell me?

15

The urgent sound of an alarm. **Billy** *and* **Martin** *on the street by the
smashed shop window.* **Billy** *is holding the green jacket. His hand is
bleeding.*

Billy For you.

Martin You smashed it.

Billy Put it on.

Martin Put your fist through a fucking window. Jesus.

Billy Put it on. Go on. It's a present.

Martin Wait. Billy . . .

Billy You said Billy.

Martin I don't want presents. I don't want to know who
you are. All I want is for you to go away. You go that way and
I'll go this way. Please.

Billy Made a brilliant noise. Didn't it? Crash.

Martin You shouldn't have done it.

Billy Take it. Take the jacket. It's yours.

Martin   I don't want it. You have it.

Billy   I chose it for you.

Martin *takes the jacket.* **Billy** *sits down on the pavement.*

Martin   Thank you.

Billy   Wear it.

Martin   Your hand.

Billy   Wear it.

Martin   You're cut.

Billy   It's a beautiful jacket. Wear it.

Martin *puts the jacket on.*

Billy   Give us a twirl.

Martin   Can you run? You run that way. Let's just run. We'll leave the jacket and run.

Billy *is sitting by the smashed window. His hand is bleeding.* **Martin** *tears a strip off the bottom of his shirt and gives it to* **Billy**.

Martin   Wrap that round your hand.

Billy   What's this? Guess this? (*American accent.*) For a minute there I thought we were in trouble.

Martin   I don't want to know.

Billy (*American accent*)   For a minute there I thought we –

Martin   Please. I'm asking. Run.

Billy   Can you guess it?

Martin   Will you run, you mad cunt?

Billy   Right. We're surrounded, by hundreds and hundreds of Mexican police, you're bandaging my hand . . . Can you guess it?

Martin   Why are you doing this?

Billy (*American*)   Wait a minute. Did you hear something?

Martin   Where?

Billy   No. It's part of the film. You have to guess.

Martin   Billy.

Billy (*American*)   For a minute there I thought we were in trouble.

Billy *enacts the final moment from* Butch Cassidy and the Sundance Kid. *He stands up, ready to spring into action, guns blazing and just as he comes out of the imaginary building he freezes and makes the sound of thousands of guns going off.*

Martin *puts his hand over* **Billy**'*s mouth. Eventually lets go of him.*

Billy   Butch Cassidy and the Sundance Kid.
Final scene. I video'd it off the telly.
That looks a bit tight around the arms, you know.
Do you want a size larger?

Martin   All right. You win. I know a place. We'll go there. Let's just get out of here before the police come.

Billy   Where? Your place?

Martin   Just a place I know. Near here. I go sometimes. Come on.

Billy *is looking at his reflection in what remains of the shop window.*

Billy   Look at us. You be Sundance. I'll be Butch.

Martin   Let's just go.

Billy (*American*)   Whaddaya mean you can't swim? The fall'll probably kill ya.

Martin   Hurry up.

Billy *takes* **Martin**'*s hand. Pretends to jump off a cliff.*

Billy   Whooooooaaaaaaah.

Looking at their reflection **Billy** *kisses* **Martin** *sexually.*

Martin   Billy.

Billy.
What are you doing?
Don't.

He pushes **Billy** *off him.*

What the fuck do you think I am?
Christ.

16

Leo *and* **Paulina**. *A dim light.* **Paulina** *is clearing up dinner plates and wiping.*

Leo   When we were first together.

She wipes around him.

I thought you were the most beautiful thing I'd ever seen.

Paulina   Are you finished?

Leo   Oh. Yes. Thank you.
Everything about you was perfect and I made sure to keep you. I thought about you all the time. About how things would be? About what I'd do . . .

She goes into the kitchen. **Leo** *lights a cigarette.*

But you start with things, you draw up plans and then they get confused. People spoil things and . . . time and you lose the clarity. So you have to get back to the original . . . go back to the drawing board.
. . .
We'll get out of the city. Paulina. A village somewhere. We'll do up a house or something. I'll work from the attic. Get back to the original us . . . all of us . . . You, me, Dorothy, Martin.

Paulina   You're smoking.

Leo   You know, Paulina, you're still a lovely looking woman.

Paulina   Put it out.

Leo   For your age. Considering. You are.

Paulina   I said you weren't to smoke here.

Leo   I want to smoke. It's a lovely night. I've had a lovely meal. Stars in a black sky and this is my lovely wife.

Paulina *takes the cigarette from his hand and stubs it out.*

Leo   I look at you sometimes and I think, I can see you when you were twenty-two.

Paulina   You said you wouldn't do that.

Leo   I can see the original, and I think . . . I want to say –

Paulina   Not in the house. I asked you.

Leo   I know you don't like me saying it but –

Paulina   Fumes and –

Leo   It doesn't stop me from wanting to say it.

Paulina   Dirt and –

Leo   I look at you and I want to say –
You're a beautiful woman.

Paulina   Ashes and –

Leo   It's pleasant just to sit here and look at you.

Paulina   Stop it, Leo.

Leo   I mean it.

Paulina   Stop.

Leo   I want to say it. I feel it.
It's objectively true.
You're beautiful.

Paulina   Leo.

Leo   My beautiful wife.

Paulina *throws a plate down onto the floor, it breaks.*

Leo   Paulina!

Paulina   Don't call me that.

Leo   Well, what do you want me to call you then?

Paulina   At the moment, nothing.

Leo   I have to call you something. I can't just point at you.

Paulina   I don't want you to refer to me.

. . .

Leo   I'm sorry. I should have offered to help with the clearing up.

. . .

Paulina, what's wrong?

Paulina   I said not to smoke.

Leo   I know, love, but after a meal, I like to . . .

Paulina   Why did I do that?

Leo   You were upset. It's understandable. I'm sorry.

Paulina   Plate throwing. It's so . . . domestic.

Leo   I'll clear it up. You sit down.

Paulina   So banal.

Leo, *on his hands and knees starts to pick up pieces of plate.* **Paulina** *sits.*

Leo   You snapped. That's all. What with Martin coming home and . . . I've not been in the best of moods. I've not helped. You snapped. It's probably a good thing.

Paulina   Such a poor gesture.

Leo   The thing is . . . we need to get things clear between us. I've let you drift away from me. We don't communicate. The two of us. In our own worlds. But we're lucky. That's what we have to remember. We're the lucky ones. We have everything . . . that's what's important to remember.

He is now standing behind her. He tries to kiss her. Her resistance is tired.

You feel so good.

Paulina   Leo.

Leo   So soft.

Paulina   Go to bed.

Leo   So lovely.

He starts trying to undress her. She is stiff. Corpse-like, she gives nothing. He continues. He kisses her breasts. She holds his head. She tolerates him.

So lovely. Such a beautiful woman. So beautiful.

17

Joe *and* **Dorothy** *in the motorway service station.*

Joe   I've got a confession to make.

Dorothy   Go on.

Joe   In the cab. I was listening to country music. Do you like country music?

Dorothy   I don't know.

Joe   Marty Robbins? Do you know Marty Robbins? El Paso? Devil Woman? White Sport Coat?
(*Sings.*) 'A white sport coat, and a pink carnation . . . I'm all dressed up, for the dance.'

Dorothy   Is that your confession?

Joe   I was listening to the song and . . .
. . .
I touched myself.
I didn't touch you.
One hand was reaching over to touch you but with the other I unzipped and –

Dorothy   Who was driving the lorry for God's sake?

Joe   We were stopped. Out there, in the lorry park. I

couldn't bear to wake you up.

. . .

Are you sure you don't want some tea?

Dorothy   Sure.

Joe   You could have me arrested.

Dorothy   Could I?

Joe   Sent to prison.

Dorothy   I've only got your word for it. I didn't see anything.

Joe   But I confessed.

Dorothy   People confess all the time. It means nothing.

Joe   Do you feel violated?

Dorothy   Do you want me to?

Joe   . . .
Yes.

Dorothy *doubles up again, holding herself as before.*

Joe   What's wrong?

Dorothy   I get attacks. It's nothing.

Joe   Attacks? Attacks of what?

Dorothy   Dread. Don't laugh at me.

Joe   I'd never.

Dorothy   I get signals. Messages. Warnings. I'm not mental.

Joe   Of course you're not.

Dorothy   Can we leave?

Joe   It could be . . . you know . . . woman-related. You've all sorts of organs down there. It could be any one of them.

Dorothy   Let's go to the lorry. Please.

Joe   These signals. Do you know where they come from?

Dorothy   No.

Joe   Maybe it's my fault.

Dorothy   No.

Joe   Maybe I'm signalling you. Maybe that's what you've been receiving. I felt something. All night maybe I've been sending out signals. Like dolphin calls across the ocean floor. Perhaps it's something like that.

He demonstrates.

Pooooooooooooow . . . Pooooooooooooow . . .
Pooooooooooow

Dorothy *laughs.*

Dorothy   Must be different frequencies, Joe. It's not your signals I'm getting. Your signals must be being picked up somewhere else.

18

Billy *and* **Martin** *on the roof of a tall building. Night.* **Billy** *is tuning a small radio. He moves around the roof searching for a signal.* **Martin** *is sitting on the edge of the roof, his legs dangling into space. Below, there is a carpet of lights stretching into the far distance. The sounds of the city float up from below, less like real noises than like memories of noises.*

The radio picks up crackles and whines, snatches of music. Eventually **Billy** *settles on a signal. A pop song. He loses it and changes position. He gains the signal again by balancing on the edge of the roof. Precariously. We hear the first bars of 'Take Me Home Country Roads' by John Denver.* **Billy** *is absolutely still . . .*

Billy   Listen.

Martin   Shhh.

Billy   Listen.

Martin   Shhh.

Billy   Martin . . .

Martin   Billy.

19

A garden in the suburbs. The wind blowing gently. Suddenly **Paulina**
*enters in some distress. She gags, holding her hand over her mouth. She
goes further into the garden. She vomits.*

20

The roof with **Billy** *and* **Martin**, *as before.*

Billy   Almost heaven . . .

Martin *tries to keep his composure.*

Billy   West Virginia.

Martin   Billy.

Billy   Blue Ridge Mountains.

Martin   Don't sing.

Billy   Shenandoah River.

Martin   I said, don't sing.

Billy   Life is old there.

Martin   Please.

Billy   Older than the trees.

Martin   Switch it off.

Billy   Younger than the mountains.

Martin   I come here for quiet.

Billy   Growing in the breeze.

Martin *tries to snatch the radio,* **Billy** *holds it out over the edge.*

Billy   Take me home.

Martin   It's supposed to be quiet.

Billy   Country roads.

Martin   You're spoiling it.

Billy   To the place.

Martin   Billy!

Billy   That I belong.

Martin   You're spoiling everything.

Billy   West Virginia.

Martin   Give me that fucking thing.

Billy   Mountain momma.

Martin   I'm warning you.

Billy   Take me home.

Martin *punches* **Billy** *hard.*

Billy   Fuck.

Billy *totters on the edge.* **Martin** *catches him. The radio falls.*

21

The garden. **Paulina** *stands in darkness, recovering.* **Leo** *enters.*

Leo   Paulina.
Where are you?
Are you there?
Paulina.
Paulina.

22

The back of a container lorry. **Dorothy** *and* **Joe** *in a half light, surrounded by barbed wire and security equipment.*

Dorothy   It's cold.

Joe   I'm sorry.

Dorothy   Isn't there any heating?

Joe   In the cab. This is just the container.

Dorothy   What's all this stuff?

Joe   Deliveries.

Dorothy   Barbed wire?

Joe   For building sites. Stops vandals. Kids'll nick anything these days. If it's not nailed down.

Dorothy   Joe . . .

Joe   If you don't want to . . .

Dorothy   I don't know.

Joe   We don't have to. We can go.

Dorothy   Kiss me.

Joe   Are you sure?

Dorothy   No.

Joe *approaches her. Cautiously he touches her face.*

Dorothy   Do you want me? Really?

Joe   Yes.

Dorothy   Say it.

Joe   I want you.

Dorothy   Don't touch me.

Joe   But . . . you said to . . .

Dorothy   Stand back. Stand there.

Joe   I'm sorry . . . I didn't mean to upset you.

Dorothy   Look at me.

A pause.

Dorothy   Do you think I'm available?

Joe   I shouldn't have asked you to do this.

Dorothy   It's an important question, Joe. Do you think I'm available?

Joe   No. Of course not.

Dorothy   It's important. Available, Joe.

Joe   . . . Yes. I don't know.

Dorothy   Look at me. What is it about me? What gives you feelings? Tell me.

Joe   This is wrong, Dorothy. This isn't working. You said you wanted.

Dorothy   Is it the clothes?

She starts to take of her dress.

Joe   Please don't.

It's cold. She holds herself awkwardly.

Dorothy   Say you want me.

Joe   I want you.

Dorothy   Say I'm yours.

Joe   You're mine.

Dorothy   What does it feel like?

Joe   Dorothy.

Dorothy   Important, Joe. What does it feel like?

Joe   I . . . you're . . . this is embarrassing, Dorothy.

Dorothy   You. Now. Tell me the feeling.

Joe   I feel ashamed. I feel disgusted.

Dorothy   By me?

Joe   This isn't what I imagined. You asked me to come with you. You seemed sure. I didn't mean . . . now you turn round and start this. I thought you –
You talked to me, didn't you?
Listened.
You wanted me.
Everything was like a dream come true and now this.
Now you're all . . .
All . . .

Dorothy   What? All what?

Joe   Just get dressed.

Dorothy   Is it my body?

Joe   Please.

Dorothy   Is my body wrong?

Joe   No.

Dorothy   Don't you want to look at it?

Joe   Not like this.

Dorothy   How then? Like this?

She takes up a page-three pose. No smile.

Joe   No!

Dorothy   You have to say. You have to tell me. How do you want me to be? How Joe?

She doubles up again. He approaches her. Holds her. Covers her up. She remains still.

23

Leo *and* **Paulina** *in the garden. Dark.* **Leo** *smoking.* **Paulina**

standing apart.

Leo   This isn't going to happen, Paulina.

Paulina   I want you to put concrete over the grass.

Leo   I won't lose you.
You have to . . .
We both –

Paulina   I don't want grass.

Leo   All of us have to stop this . . . falling apart that's
happening here.

Paulina   I want a patio.

Leo   This is my family.
Families have problems. It's natural. You expect it.

Paulina   Leave a space for the roses.

Leo   But you can't just . . .
You have to pull things back together.

Paulina   All the rest concrete.

24

The roof. **Billy** *and* **Martin**.

Martin   Sorry.

Billy   Been hit worse before.

Martin   You kept going.

Billy   Not even a hit really. A slap it was. Not a punch. I've
had it harder than that.

Martin   I don't hit people. Not normally. Not for pleasure.

Billy   It was all right.

Martin   Don't.

Billy   Motherly, almost.

Martin   For God's sake.

Billy   Warm. Nice.

Martin   I said I was sorry.

Billy   No need.

Martin   I come up here to get away from . . . for silence.
Because it's pure. No voices. No talking.

Billy   I came up for you. I'm the one who should be sorry.

Martin   Twenty floors up you'd think there'd be nothing.
No people, no sound, no signals, no feelings.
And then you.
I had it. Just for a moment.
And then you.

Billy   I spoiled it.

Martin   Blankness. Purity. And then that trash.

Billy   Steady on. I like John Denver.

Martin   That isn't the point.

Billy   I think John Denver is pure.

Martin   Pollution.

Billy   Looks almost like the Milky Bar kid.

Martin   We could have fucked.
We could have.
Us, alone, no mess.
You spoiled it.

Billy   You're upset.

Martin   Yes.

Billy   I thought it was how we were feeling.
I thought it was romantic. Our song.
I've always wanted an 'our song' with someone.
We could have danced.
Like in a film.

Martin I don't want something that's like in a film.
Something that's like in a film is exactly what I don't want.
I wanted to slip away.

Billy From what?

Martin You. Me. Everything.

Billy If you'd told me.

Martin It was a perfect moment.

Billy There'll be another. They probably happen all the
time up here. Regular.

Martin What do you know about perfect moments?

Billy I know.

Martin How?

Billy I just had one then.

25

The inside of the lorry. The engine is turning over. **Dorothy** *and* **Joe**
are parked outside her house.

Dorothy I'd better go.

Joe . . .

Dorothy I've got work tomorrow.

Joe . . .

Dorothy I'm sorry it didn't . . .
I'm sorry I wasn't . . .

Joe . . .

Dorothy You weren't to know about me.
I don't know about me.
I'm not nice.
I led you on. Didn't I?

Joe   . . .

Dorothy   Will you see me again? Send signals.
Poooooow . . .
Will you stop for me?

Joe   . . .

Dorothy   Goodbye, Joe.

She kisses his cheek and gets out of the cab.

*We see **Paulina** standing in the garden.*

*We see **Leo**.*

*We see **Billy** and **Martin** standing on the roof. **Martin** is standing behind **Billy** holding his head.*

Leo   I won't let you drift away, Paulina.

Billy   You can see my house from here.

Leo   We're a good family.

Billy   Martin.
I said you can see . . .

Martin *lets go of **Billy**'s head.*

Martin   What makes you think I care where you live?

Leo   I won't let you put up walls between us.

Paulina   You're the architect, Leo.

Billy *suddenly turns and runs full tilt at the edge of the roof.*

Martin   Billy!

Martin *tries to catch him, he has to run full speed after him. They both run towards the edge.*

Blackout.

Act Two

1

Darkness.

Lights suddenly up on **Billy** *being caught by* **Martin** *just as he is about to go over the edge.*

Martin   You cunt.

Martin *holds* **Billy***, limply, despairing. In the background we hear a large series of explosions. The sound of applause. Lights down.*

2

Some weeks later.

The garden is in a mess. It has been dug up, ploughed and turned over. There are only scattered patches of green. A pile of concrete paving stones are stacked against the wall of the house. **Leo** *is paving over the garden.*

Paulina *enters carrying plant pots. She begins to transfer plants from the garden into pots. She watches him.*

Leo   Working.

Paulina   I can see.

Leo   It seems a shame to –

Paulina   It's what I want.

Leo   Yes, I know, love, but –

Paulina   You can sweep patios.

Leo   To cover it all though –

Paulina   Wash them.

Leo   It'll take value off the house.
People like a garden.

Paulina   I don't want you trailing dirt inside.

Leo   But when . . . if we move. When we go to the country . . . it seems a shame.

Paulina   Hose yourself down when you're finished.

Martin *comes out. Dressed for going out. He is wearing the green jacket. A pause.*

Martin   You'll kill him.

Paulina   Is that what you're wearing?

Martin   I've been watching from the bedroom.

Paulina   Are you going somewhere?

Martin   All that sweating.

Paulina   Somewhere you want to attract attention?

Martin   Manual labour. He's not used to it. You'll put a strain on his heart.

Paulina   You should be careful.

Martin   I'm going out.

Paulina   Clothes send signals.

Martin   He's been at it all afternoon.

Paulina   There are people, Martin, who interpret signals. One way or another.

Martin   It's a labour of love.

Paulina   Signals attract them.

Martin   He's moving the earth for you.

Paulina   These people.

Martin   Is the earth moving for you?

Paulina   Even if you don't actually talk to them. They come into your proximity. You should be careful.

Martin   You got another spade, boss?

Leo   ...

Martin   Give us it.

Leo   What for?

Martin   I can just see myself as a digger.

Leo *gives* **Martin** *the spade.* **Martin** *takes his jacket off. They dig together.*

Paulina   I thought you were going out.

Martin   I decided to work instead.

Leo   You could dig there if you want.

Paulina   You'll have to throw away your good clothes.

Martin   Father and son together in honest toil.

Paulina   You'll spoil them.

Martin   Good this, isn't it, boss?

Leo   What?

Martin   Digging.

Paulina   You don't both have to do it.

Martin   You and me. Digging together.

Paulina   It only means two sets of dirt.

Martin   I could dig roads in Canada or something.

Leo   You don't dig roads. You build them.

Martin   Digging's involved though. The company of digging men.

Leo   They use earth movers.

Martin   I could dig.

Leo   Nowadays road building's all about planning.

Paulina   You'll want beer.

Leo   Ask yourself what the road's for.

Paulina   When you do father and son things you always want beer.

Leo   A beer would be nice.

Paulina   There isn't any.

Leo   You ask yourself. Who's going to use this road? Why? What do they need? How can it be more beautiful? That's what the job's about, that's what men like me, and you, are for, Martin . . . we ask questions . . . you understand?

They dig for some moments in silence.

Martin   Actually, I'm bored of this.

Martin *stops.*

Leo   You've only just started.

Martin   Sorry.

Leo (*to* **Paulina**)   I thought you were getting beers.

Martin   For a minute I thought I would –
But then I seemed to get bored.

Leo   He wants a beer.

Martin   Digging wasn't that interesting after all.

Leo   That's what I'm telling you. It's the planning that's interesting, the questions . . .

Martin   Sorry, Boss.
Maybe I'm just not cut out for work.
I have to go.

Paulina   You're not coming into the house.

Martin   I'll be late.

Leo   Martin.

Martin   See you later.

Martin *exits through the house.*

Leo   You could have given him a drink.

Paulina   He didn't want a drink.

Leo   Of course he did. It's a warm day. He wanted a cold beer. I want a cold beer.

Paulina   You wanted a beer. He wanted to dig.

. . .

Do you know they use fish brains in beer?

Leo   Fish heads.

Paulina   No wonder it makes people violent.
Men urinating in the street.
Women stumbling around like retarded people.
Considering what they put in it, it's no wonder.

They hear the sound of the doorbell. Neither of them move. After a moment **Dorothy** *enters.*

Dorothy   There's a woman here to see you.

Leo   Who?

Paulina   A woman?

Dorothy   Mackie she said.

Leo   Christ.

Dorothy   Will I tell her you're busy?

Leo   No. No. Bring her through.

Dorothy *exits.*

Leo   Business.

Paulina   Shame.

Sheena *enters with* **Dorothy**.

Sheena   This is lovely. What a lovely house you've got, Mr Black. Did you build it?

Leo   No.

Sheena   And this is your . . . backyard?

Dorothy   It's a patio actually.

Sheena   For sitting out?

Paulina   It's easier to clean.

Sheena   Of course it is. I'd love a patio. You don't get much chance to sit out where I am. You must be Mrs Black.

Paulina   Paulina.

Sheena   Sheena Mackie.

Leo   You always seem to find me at weekends, Ms Mackie.

Sheena   I've got a job. I have to work in the week. And this is your daughter?

Dorothy   Dorothy.

Sheena   The girl I talked to on the phone?

Leo   Dorothy is also my secretary.

Sheena   A family business. That's nice. We hardly need to be introduced, do we? We've chatted so often.

Leo   Why don't you get us some tea, Dorothy? If you'll allow me to get changed, Ms Mackie, I'll be with you in a moment.

Leo and **Dorothy** exit. **Paulina** continues potting plants. **Sheena** stands silent.

Paulina   I've always thought it would be nice to live in a tall building.

Sheena   Oh?

Paulina   Is it nice?

Sheena   Nice? Not really. Not nice. No.

Paulina   Are you scared of heights?

Sheena   Height's not really the problem.

Paulina   Oh no. Height's a strong point. You don't want to be in amongst it.

Sheena   Amongst it?

Paulina   Ground floors attract opportunist thieves. I don't imagine they bother with the tenth. On the tenth you can watch it all happening down below. Rise above it all. Do you watch?

Sheena   Sometimes. Sometimes I can't avoid it. Sometimes I'm in amongst it myself.

3

Billy *and* **Martin** *on top of a tall building. Daytime.* **Billy** *pointing.*

Billy   There . . . to the left.

Martin   Where?

Billy   Follow my finger.

Martin   There's only tower blocks.

Billy   That's it . . . there see.

Martin   There?

Billy   Third along.

Martin   You live there?

Billy   Yeah.

Martin   Christ.

Billy   What d'you mean, Christ?

Martin   I mean . . . Christ. Isn't it supposed to be . . . I've never been. I thought you were showing because . . .

Billy   I'm showing you because it's where I live.

Martin   I've never. I haven't seen any of those places . . . close up. I mean.

Billy   Where do you live?

Martin   You can't see it from here.

Billy   Is it a flat?

Martin   No.

Billy   A house.

Martin   Yes.

Billy   Is it detached or part of a street?

Martin   Detached. Do we have to talk about this?

Billy   Nice area?

Martin   If you like nice areas.

Billy   Can I visit?

Martin   When I was a student I lived in a squat.

Billy   Can I visit?

Martin   No.

Billy *starts to walk along the edge of the roof. Calmly balancing.*

Billy   Why not? You can visit me.

Martin   So. Don't do that.

Billy   Visit me. On my dangerous estate.

Martin   You'll fall off.

Billy   It's like Beirut you know. War zone.

Martin   Is it?

Billy   Is it fuck.

Martin   I said don't do that.

Billy   You're scared.

Martin   Probably better than where I stay anyway.

Billy   How's that?

Martin   I don't know. It probably is.

Billy   How's it better?

Martin   The people probably. Probably the atmosphere.
Isn't it supposed to be better. Neighbours talk to each other I
don't know. How should I know?

. . .

Will you fucking stop doing that? It makes me nervous.

Billy *stops walking along the roof edge.*

Billy   Can I visit yours then?

Martin   I won't be there long anyway.

Billy   You moving?

Martin   Leaving.

Billy   Leaving what?

Martin   Home. I can't stick it.
The city. The country. All of it.
I'm off.

Billy   Where to?

Martin   Canada. I don't know. Albania maybe. Maybe Fife.
Some wilderness. Somewhere with mountains.

Billy   A holiday?

Martin   Escape.

Billy   What have you got to escape from?

Martin   You wouldn't understand.

Billy   Maybe I would.

Martin   I need a change.

Billy   I like you as you are.

Martin   You're shit, you'll take anything.

Billy   I take what I want.

Martin   I'm fucking off. On my own. No people. No talk.
No things.

Billy   I'll come with you.

Martin   No, you won't.

Billy   Why not?

Martin   I don't want you to come.

Billy   Yes, you do.

Martin   You'd only talk. When people talk they clog your head with shit. The shit they talk gets in your head and slops around. More and more shit. Television schedules. Opinions about sport. Property prices. It all slops around until eventually it slops out your mouth and back into someone else's head.

Billy   You're fucked up?

Martin   Course I'm fucked up.

Billy   We've got something in common then. I'm fucked up as well.

Martin   No, you're not.

Billy   I try to run off the top of buildings.

Martin   That's natural. You're poor.
. . .
I just can't . . . I'm not . . . not any more.
. . .
I need to get pure. I got off on the wrong foot somewhere. Somewhere around when I was born. Now I need to go back. Go back get clean and start again.
. . .
I'm going to learn to make furniture.

Billy   I'd like to do that.

Martin   If I go to the country somewhere. I could find some old guy in the mountains that does it.

Billy   Yeah!

Martin   An old guy with a fat old wife.

Billy   Yeah!

Martin   He might be deaf. A deaf couple.

Billy   An apprentice.

Martin   He'll show me what to do with signs. I'll learn how to turn wood and make tables.

Billy   The two of us.

Martin   I'm going alone.
I've got it all planned. I'm just going to set off and walk.
Just head in that direction and not stop.

He points.

Billy   That's the sea.

Martin   That way then.

Billy   Bathgate. No mountains there.

Martin   Fuck off.

Billy   I'll follow you.

Martin   I'll run.

Billy   I'll chase you.

Martin   I'll kill you.

Billy   Have you told your mum and dad?

Martin   I'll leave a note.

Billy   They'll worry.

Martin   It's for the best.

Billy   They'll be hurt.

Martin   Don't try and tell me what they'll feel. You haven't a fucking clue.

Billy   Neither have you.

Martin   I know exactly what they'll feel. I know precisely.
I can feel it for them. Better than them.
They'll feel pain.
A great amount of pain.

Billy   So stay.

Martin   I don't like them.

Billy   So. Stick it.

Martin   The longer I stay the more I want to hurt them.

Billy   Everyone gets that. That's not special.

Martin   Stay or go. Makes no difference. Either way there'll
be a great amount of pain.

Billy   Martin.
I don't want you to go without me.

Martin   You can't come.

Billy   I'll miss you.

Martin   So.

Billy   I'll feel a great amount of pain.

Martin   You attached yourself to me. If you attach yourself
to someone like me you deserve pain. I have to go away and
make furniture for a while. If I make furniture in a lonely
place for long enough then maybe, I'll become a good person.

Billy   You believe that?

Martin   Of course I fucking don't.

Billy   Why say it then?

Martin   It's the only thing I can think of.

Billy *takes* **Martin**'s *head in his hands, suddenly. Turns his face
towards him.*

Martin   Fuck off.

Billy   Look at me.

Martin   Stop it.

Billy   Look at me.

Martin *is struggling but* **Billy** *is stronger. He holds on.* **Martin**
gives up struggling.

Billy   I can make you good.

Me.

You cunt.

Me.

Billy.

Understand?

I can make you good.

Billy *lets go.*

4

Sheena, **Paulina**, **Leo** *and* **Dorothy** *inside the house. A model of Eden Court is on the table by* **Leo**. **Sheena** *is examining the model.*

Sheena   This one's mine.

Leo   I realise the current fashion's against high-rise building, Mrs Mackie.

Sheena   Sheena.

Leo   Of course, Sheena. Dorothy. Will you offer Sheena some tea?

Dorothy *doesn't move.*

Sheena   Wait a minute. Is it this one? One balcony's much the same as any other, isn't it? Have you put all the windows in?

Leo   Paulina, you don't need to stay. If you don't want to. This is work.

Paulina   I'm interested.

Sheena   It could be any one of these. It depends on which way round you stand.

Paulina   I'm interested in your buildings.

Leo   Fine. Whatever.

Sheena   Something's different. The shape of it . . . colour or something.

Leo   It's an exact model, Mrs Mackie, an exact model of the
Eden Court design. I wanted you to see this to make a point.

Sheena   The grass. You've made the grass green. Put green
felt down.

Dorothy   That's the convention. All models do that.

Leo   This is the original design. Six standing towers. Aerial
walkways linking each tower, platforms linking each balcony.
The whole enclosing a central park.

Sheena   It shouldn't be green. That part of the estate's all
mud now. It catches the rain. It's like a draining bowl. You
want to put down brown felt for that.

Dorothy   The models aren't supposed to be realistic.
They're impressions.

Leo   The original design was, in fact, loosely based on
Stonehenge.

Paulina   I didn't think anyone lived in Stonehenge.

Leo   Standing stones were the inspiration.

Paulina   Too draughty I thought.

Sheena   Didn't you win an award for this?

Dorothy   He did.

Leo   I won some recognition at the time.

Sheena   It looks good. From this angle. From above.

Dorothy   It's about space. Architecture's about shaping
space. If you look at it from here you can see how he's
moulding a communal space.

Sheena   Were the judges in a helicopter when they gave you
the award?

Leo   I was asked to build cheap homes. Cheap housing.
High density accommodation. Eden Court is a council estate,
Mrs Mackie, but I built connecting areas, and public spaces, I
designed it so everyone's front room gets the sun at certain

times of the day. They're not luxury homes, but
architecturally, they're well designed. That's the point I'm
making. I put as much imagination, as much thought, as
much of my self into these buildings as any –

Dorothy   I think they're beautiful.

Leo   Objectively, aesthetically, functionally . . . Eden Court
is a good estate.

Sheena   People are queueing up to leave.

Dorothy   It's a free country.

Sheena   They're unhappy. They get depressed. They get ill.
The place they live in makes them depressed.
Do you understand that?
Do you understand how important that is?

Leo   It's mass housing. You can't build mass housing to suit
individual desires. It doesn't matter who designs it. You can
knock it down if you want to but the problems will still be
there. There'll still be unemployment, there'll still be poverty.
If you want to change your circumstances Mrs Mackie –

Sheena   Sheena.

Leo   I suggest you vote Labour.
I do.

Sheena   Would you say Eden Court was yours? Your
building?

Leo   I designed it.

Sheena   Would you say it was your responsibility?

Leo   It was my responsibility. It's not my fault the council
turned it into a ghetto. I didn't put the people in it.

Sheena   Were you there when the flats were built?

Leo   I supervised the project.

Sheena   Did you actually supervise the work? Watch every
bolt go in? See every panel in place?

Leo   Of course not.

Sheena   Build them high, build them quick and build them cheap. That was the idea, wasn't it?

Leo   Not my idea.

Sheena   No, but it was the commission, wasn't it . . . what you were told?

Leo   They were designed to be built easily.

Sheena   Built in factories. Pre-cast.

Leo   It's a simple method.

Sheena   Easy to skimp on as well. Difficult to check up on mistakes.

Leo   I didn't hire the contractors.

Sheena   A few bolts missing here and there. They always over-design these things anyway. If the odd panel doesn't fit, never mind.

Leo   I admit there was a lack of supervision but the contractors were under pressure. Time was a pressure. You may not remember but it was you people who were demanding the houses.

Paulina   That's not how I remember it.

Leo   What?

Paulina   I remember you talking about it. At the time. You said the job was rushed. You said it was a scandal.

Leo   I'm not sure you know what you're talking about, Paulina.

Paulina   She does.

Sheena   I don't mean to seem rude, Mr Black. You're probably a nice man. You've a nice family. You probably meant for it to be a nice place to live. Isn't that what architects are for? I remember the brochures we got. A drawing of the sun shining and kids playing in the park. When they came round looking for tenants I signed like that. I saw the models. But it was all 'vision', wasn't it? Vision's the word you would use. Not houses, but a vision of housing. Everyone nicely boxed away. Cheaply accommodated. Eden Court might look like Stonehenge to you, it might have won an award but it's build like a pack of cards.

Leo It's secure. It won't fall down.

Sheena Boxes piled one on top of the other and we're stuffed in them like exhibits. You weren't asked to design houses, you were asked to house people, there's a world of difference.

Dorothy That's rubbish. It's rubbish. I've already told her she's talking rubbish, Dad.

Leo Dorothy, I think you've said enough.

Sheena The local authority can't afford to admit the mistakes. The contractors have money. They'd probably be happy to go to court. The whole thing could take years. We don't have years. We're just ordinary people who would like decent places to live. If you give us your support they can't ignore us.

Leo I won't lie about my own building.

Sheena It's not your building though, is it? It never was. You just did the frippery bits that win prizes. Your stuff's just the façade. Take it away and the place is a dormitory block. Stonehenge, communal space, it doesn't mean anything if there isn't life in the place – shops, work, kids, pubs.

Leo There was supposed to be.

Sheena But there wasn't.

Leo So destroy it. Blame the building. Wipe it out.

Sheena Architecture's for the people who pay. Always. All we want to do is take control. It's not about good or bad buildings, it's about who decides. Don't we have the right to not like good buildings? You do.

Leo   I think we're agreed this is not my problem.

Sheena   But you can solve it.

Leo   I don't see why I should.

Sheena   Because it would be a good thing.

Leo   I can't help you. I'm sorry. I won't see good ideas blown up just because some people can't see beyond their own misery.

Paulina   I think you should knock them down.

Dorothy   Mum.

Paulina   If that's what people want.
At least they know what they want.
If they're sure. Then it's cruel, isn't it?
To stop them just because of history, or how things were supposed to be. The intention.
I think you should help them.

Leo   This is about work, Paulina. This is about destroying my work.

Sheena   I'm sorry you couldn't help us.
If you change your mind you know where to find me.

Paulina   Don't go. Why don't you stay . . . for lunch.
I was making lunch.

Sheena   Thank you but . . . I think I should go.
I can find my own way out.

Sheena *leaves.*

Leo   You're supposed to support me.

Paulina   I thought she was right. I thought she won the argument.

Leo   That isn't the point. You're my wife.

Paulina *leaves.*

Leo   Well, you can forget your fucking patio.

Paulina.
You can forget your fucking patio.
Do you hear me?

Dorothy Don't worry about it, Dad. She's mad.
Nobody's going to knock it down.
Anyone can see she's mad.

Leo Why didn't you give me her letters?

Dorothy They were rubbish. I told you.

Leo Why didn't you give me them?

Dorothy I told you . . . They were just . . . I didn't want
you to worry.

Leo What's wrong with you, Dorothy?

Dorothy Dad.

Leo Did you think I'd made a mistake?

Dorothy I thought –

Leo I'm your father, Dorothy. I'm your employer.
How dare you humiliate me like that.
Did you think I'd built it badly?

Dorothy No.

Leo Did you think that was possible?

Dorothy Please.

Leo There was no mistake.

Dorothy I know.

Leo The structure is sound.

Dorothy I know.

Leo No mistake.

Leo *picks up the model and leaves the room. A wave of nausea passes
over* **Dorothy**. **Paulina** *enters.*

Paulina Are you sick?

Dorothy   No.

Paulina   You look like you're going to be sick.

Dorothy   I'm all right.

Paulina   Shall I bring water?

Dorothy   I'm not going to be sick.

Paulina   You're not pregnant, are you?

Dorothy   What?

Paulina   If you've got nausea.

Dorothy   I'm not pregnant.

Paulina   How do you know?

Dorothy   I know.

Paulina   Did you test yourself?

Dorothy   I know.

Paulina   Maybe you should test yourself.
You look pale.
Your complexion's . . .
There's a spot. It might be hormonal.

Dorothy   Why did you do that, Mum?

Paulina   Do what?

Dorothy   Behave like that. In front of that woman. Why?

Paulina   How did I behave?

Dorothy   As though you were neurotic. You behaved as
though you were neurotic.

Paulina   I only said –

Dorothy   He was humiliated. In front of –

Paulina   I only said . . .

Dorothy   In front of everyone . . .

Paulina   I was commenting on . . .

Dorothy   You made him look small.

Paulina   What she said. The woman.

Dorothy   In front of . . .

Paulina   It made sense.

Dorothy   In front of me.
You didn't need to –
There was no need.

Paulina   I'm sorry. I didn't mean –

Dorothy   Tell him that. Say sorry to him.

Paulina *approaches* **Dorothy**. *Tries to touch her.*

Paulina   Dorothy.

Dorothy   Why do you have to make him . . .
Why can't you be decent to him?
You used to be decent to him.

Paulina   It's difficult . . .

Dorothy   Try.

Paulina   It's complicated. You wouldn't –

Dorothy   Explain.

Paulina   I really think it's best left between –

Dorothy   Tell me.

Paulina   I don't see what's to be gained from digging
around in –

Dorothy   Tell me.

Paulina   In exploring this . . . landscape. Really, it's not
interesting. I promise you. This situation between your father
and me. It's quite . . .

Dorothy   What?

Paulina   Mundane.

Dorothy What?

Paulina I have no . . .
So embarrassing really.
No admiration for him.

Pause. **Dorothy** *turns away from her. Silent. Holding back tears.*

Paulina No feeling . . .

Dorothy Not good enough.

Paulina It stopped. It just finished.

Dorothy Not good enough.

Paulina I look at him now. I can't bear to –

Dorothy Selfish.

Paulina The way he –

Dorothy Selfish.

Paulina He looks so . . . failed.

Dorothy Selfish cow. You're a –

Paulina It's not like that.

Dorothy Selfish bloody cow.
Selfish self-centred bloody cow.
. . .
Sorry.

Paulina It can change, Dorothy. It can just . . .

Dorothy He's the same. He's the same man.
He needs you.

Paulina I know.
But it can't be like that any more.
I'm sorry.
. . .
You look pale.

Dorothy I'm fine.

Paulina You need to look after yourself.

Dorothy   I'm all right.

Paulina   If you worry, if you upset yourself, it shows in your skin, you know. It shows itself.

Dorothy   Mum, please, just leave me alone.

Paulina   You used to have such a clear complexion. Hot water. A glass of hot water. Every evening. It's cleansing. It has a cleansing effect.

Dorothy   Go away, Mum. Please.

Paulina   You know it's not my fault. Don't you, Dorothy?

Dorothy   What does that mean?

Paulina   Nothing. It means it's not my fault.

5

Darkness. The sound of a motorway. Traffic passing. **Dorothy** *is hitching. Lights pass her but no one stops.*

6

Martin *and* **Billy** *on a muddy patch of grass in Eden Court.* **Martin** *is wearing the green jacket.*

Billy   This is it. This is where I'm from.

Martin   Nice.

Billy   Don't look so nervous.

Martin   I'm not nervous.

Billy   Your hands are shaking.

Billy *touches his hand.*

Martin   Piss off.

A sudden bang. It echoes. **Martin** *throws himself to the ground.*

Billy   Air-gun.

Martin   I wasn't. I just wanted to sit down.

Billy   You'll spoil your jacket. You don't know what you'll pick up.

Martin   Seems all right to me.

Billy   Eight blocks. They're all the same. In a big circle. You're supposed to be able to tell the time from the shadows.

Martin   Can you?

Billy   I don't know. I can only tell the time digital. Apparently the architect committed suicide when he saw how it turned out. It's supposed to be built backwards or something. Probably found out it told the time backwards and topped himself.
So what do you think?

Martin   Can't you leave?

Billy   Not unless I'm thrown out. If I got thrown out I could be rehoused.

Martin   You could get a job.

Billy   So could you.

Martin   I don't want one.

Billy   Neither do I.

Martin   I thought you wanted to work. I thought that was the problem. I thought you people wanted jobs.

Billy   We have to say that.

Martin   I thought . . .

Billy   Why should I want a job? You don't. I couldn't put up with this place and a job as well. I'd die.

Martin   So what d'you do all day?

Billy   I'm like one of those flies. You know those flies that are born and breed and die all in one day but to the fly that day's a lifetime? That's me. Skating across the water for an afternoon.

Martin   I don't know how you can stand it.

Billy   I didn't say I could.

Martin   I don't know how anyone could.

Billy   Maybe we're a new species. Like the cockroaches.

Martin   Why did you bring me here?

Billy   It's where I'm from. I wanted you to see.

Martin   Are you trying to make some point?

Billy   No.

Martin   Make me feel something.

Billy   Martin, we could go somewhere. Both of us. We could both just . . . fuck off.
If we went away together.

Martin   We won't.

Billy   But if we did. We could even go abroad. You've got money. I could work. In a foreign country I could work. We could just get on a train now. Get on a train and fuck off to the sunshine. You and me.

Martin   No.

Billy   Think about it. Greece. Spain. Italy. Amsterdam. You and me. People think about it but nobody does it. We could make furniture together.

Martin   Making furniture was my idea.

Billy   I could have my own idea.

Martin   You took me here to say this, didn't you?

Billy   Think about it. We could learn the language. Eat the food. Work. Sun. Dress in Italian clothes. We could do it.

Martin   You had it all planned.

Billy   Think about it.

Martin   Make me feel bad. Make me save you.

Billy   It's not like that. It's an idea.

Martin   What do you think I am?
The White Knight of the Lavatories?
Sir Galahad of The Gents?

Billy   You need me.

Martin   In your dreams.

Billy   I like you, Martin.

Martin   So?

Billy   Nobody else does.

7

Dorothy *is sitting in her bedroom, in front of the mirror, in her under-wear.* **Leo** *enters without knocking.* **Dorothy** *instinctively covers up.*

Leo   Oh. I'm sorry. Can I come in?

Dorothy   Dad.

Leo   I just thought I'd . . .

Dorothy   Do you want the seat?

Leo   I'll crouch. That's what I'll do. I'll crouch beside you.
Dorothy, I . . .

He reaches out to touch her and then withdraws his hand.

I'm sorry about earlier on.

Dorothy   It's fine.

Leo   I shouldn't have shouted. I was.

Dorothy   Honestly, it's fine.

Leo   You know I love you.

Dorothy   Do you want a drink?

Leo   Sorry?

Dorothy   A lemonade? I want a lemonade. I made some.
Do you want me to get you one?

Dorothy *is about to get up and go.*

Leo   Wait. It's all right.

Dorothy   I'll get that drink, shall I?

Leo   I need to know something.
You and I . . .
We do . . . like each other, don't we?

Dorothy   I'm parched actually. (*She coughs.*)

Leo   We're friends.

Dorothy   Friends. Yes.

Leo   You're sure?

Dorothy   Course I'm sure. I think I will have that lemonade
after all.

Leo   Don't go yet.

Dorothy   Whatever.

Leo   You see, Dorothy.
This is difficult for me to say.
But . . .
I feel slightly . . . alone.
At the moment.

Dorothy   Oh.

Leo   I'm telling you this because . . .
Well, because things are . . .
Martin . . . your mother. I can't seem to talk to them . . .

Dorothy   I told you. You're my dad.

Leo   I want you to know that I love you.

Dorothy   Dad, I'm sorry. I don't want to seem. It's your business, isn't it? You and Mum. I'm glad you feel you can talk to me. I love you. You love me. It's difficult to talk about that sort of thing so the effort is . . . appreciated. But you don't have to say it. That's the nice thing about families, isn't it? You just know. You don't always have to say.

Leo   Martin isn't going to work for me, is he? He's going to go away.

Dorothy   You don't know.

Leo   As a father sometimes.
You think you might have made the wrong choices.
You want to ask.

Dorothy   He said he was interested.

Leo   No.

Dorothy   Time. He needs –

Leo   You think if you could go back . . .
I've been thinking . . .
If I could go back.
Go back to the point where the mistake happened.

Dorothy   Oh God.

Leo   What?

Dorothy   I can't.

Leo   Can't what?

Dorothy   This conversation.
Can't do it. Sorry.

Leo   I feel lost, Dorothy.
I've no plans for this.
It's not part of the design.
Tell me the truth, Dorothy . . .
Does he hate me?
Does he despise me?

Dorothy   As a matter of fact I feel very thirsty now.

She puts on her dressing-gown and leaves.

8

The sudden, loud blast of a lorry's horn. **Joe** *is in his cab driving. The radio is turned up loud. It is playing 'From Boulder to Birmingham' sung by Emmylou Harris.* **Joe** *is playing with the steering wheel.*

Joe   Pooooow Pooooow Pooooow.

9

Martin *and* **Billy** *in a gay bar. In the background a pub quiz is going on.*

Martin   Stop sulking. You took me here. I got you a drink. Fucking drink it.

Paulina *and* **Leo** *have just had sex.* **Leo** *is still in the bed.* **Paulina** *is sitting nearby.*

Leo   Do you mind if I have a cigarette?
. . .
It's been a long time.
. . .

Voice   Number Fifteen.
Pencils at the ready. Boys and Girls.
Who played the male and female leads in a. *Pretty Woman*, b. *Pretty in Pink* and c. *Pink Flamingos*?

Billy   Richard Gere, Julia Roberts . . .

Martin   You know that?

Billy   Put the answers down.

Leo *lights up a cigarette.*

Leo   I'm glad it happened. It needed to happen. I'm glad you . . .

Paulina   It was interesting.

Leo   More than interesting.

Martin *and* **Billy**.

Martin   I can't believe you know that.

Billy   Hand it in.

Paulina *and* **Leo**.

Paulina   It was an experiment. The results were interesting.

Leo   An experiment? You're my wife.

Paulina   I wish you wouldn't call me that.

Leo   Christ, not this again.

Paulina   Wife, it's so bovine. Husband. It's all so agricultural.

Billy *and* **Martin**.

Voice   Staying with pretty women . . . who had a hit with 'Oh Pretty Woman' . . . there are options in this question.

Billy   Roy Orbison.

Voice   You may prefer to wait for your options.

Billy   It's Roy Orbison.

Martin   He said you may prefer . . .

Billy   Just put it down.

Voice   Just to remind you, boys and girls, the prizes tonight are champagne, a bottle of crème de menthe and a five-pound voucher for I.G. Mellis.

Billy *has written the answer.*

Billy   Give it in.

Leo *and* **Paulina**.

Leo   Paulina.

Paulina   Have you noticed? When you can't think of anything else to say you say 'Paulina'.

Leo   Why are you spoiling this?

Paulina   You want me to be touched. Moved. As though your voice making that sound might stir me up.

Leo   Doesn't it?

Paulina   No. That's the interesting thing. Paulina. It feels like it isn't my name any more. Feels more connected with you now than with me.

Leo   What then?
What can I say to stir you up?

Paulina   Dressing-table. Bedroom. Husband. Living-room. Sofa. Carpet. Wall.

Leo   What?

Paulina   Window. Floor. Laundry basket.

Leo   Paulina.

Paulina   Dinner party. Garden. Cheeseboard. Paulina.

Leo   Are you having a breakdown? Is that what this is?

Paulina   Making love. Making love.

Leo   I thought you wanted . . . You asked me.

Paulina   You find yourself amongst these words.
You find these words being used.
You begin to notice. People say them without blinking.

Leo   You've lost me. You have to explain this.

Paulina   Everyone wants me to explain.

Leo   We go to bed in the middle of the afternoon. It's wonderful. We make up. Everything's better and then you start having some kind of breakdown. You could at least try to explain . . .

Paulina   I have to ask you to leave Leo.

Leo   . . .

Paulina   The house. I mean.

Leo   What the hell am I supposed to have done?

Paulina   I realise it's your house as much as it's mine. More maybe. But I'd like you to leave it. Would you do that for me? As a gesture of affection. You're not an unusually cruel man. You'd be better at living somewhere else than me.

Leo   For Christ's sake. It's not gone that far, has it?

Paulina   It will.

Leo   A trial separation.

Paulina   Not trial. A separation.

Leo   You want to throw away a marriage. Just like that.

Paulina   Not 'throw away'. Those are the wrong words.

Leo   I'm sorry. I don't have a thesaurus.

Paulina   If you could throw it away, forget it, start again etc. All those things but . . . go back to a time before it happened and follow a different route but . . . wherever I go now, for the rest of my life I'll take this marriage with me. For better or worse. I'm not throwing it away.

Leo   Why now? More than twenty years you've had, and now, today you say it's a mistake . . . why not yesterday, why not years ago?

Paulina   Fear.

Leo   Fear? Afraid of me? Don't make me laugh.

Paulina   Afraid of me. Afraid there wasn't any of me left. Afraid I'd eroded.
. . .
I am trying, Leo . . .
Does that explain it?

Leo   No, it fucking doesn't.

Paulina Don't you feel it? Feel yourself eroding?

Leo No. No, I don't.

Paulina Really?

Leo Really.

Paulina That's interesting.

Billy *and* **Martin**.

Billy Wait a minute wait . . .
Ahhh . . . It's coming . . .
Rick Alessi.
Rick Alessi, Sharon Watts and Sinbad.

Martin *writes the answers down.*

Martin How can you fill your head with this shit?
I can't believe this amount of shit can be in one head.

Billy Just put the answer in.

Martin Why don't we go somewhere else?

Billy I'm winning.

Voice Born in 1908, Indiana, Pennsylvania. No longer alive
or active in the field in which he or she first found fame.

Billy Fuck.

Martin I'm leaving.

Billy Film star. Film star . . . think . . .

Martin I said, let's go.

Leo *and* **Paulina**.

Leo I'm sorry.

Paulina Don't apologise.

Leo I'm sorry.

Paulina You haven't done anything wrong.

Leo I didn't see.

Paulina   You're just part of a situation.

Billy *and* **Martin**.

Billy   Bette Davis!

Martin   You coming then.

Billy   Wait though, too early for Bette Davis.

Leo *and* **Paulina**.

Paulina   You're part of a situation that developed. That's all. Not your fault.

Leo   I mean more to you than that.
I think you forget sometimes, Paulina, that I know you.
I know you better than anyone.

Paulina   You know your wife. When you leave you'll notice a wife-shaped space.

Billy *and* **Martin**.

Voice   You may want to wait for your options.

Billy   Leave if you want to.

Martin   You haven't finished your drink.

Leo *and* **Paulina**.

Leo   We need to have fun again. That's all it is. We stopped having fun. Kids and everything. Responsibility. Changes you. We need to rekindle . . . get back, and . . . I can't believe you feel nothing. I can't believe there's nothing there.

Paulina   There's knowledge. I know you. Knowledge and a sort of disgust. The sort of disgust a prisoner feels for a cell mate. That's all.

Billy *and* **Martin**.

Billy   Jimmy Stewart!

Martin   What?

Billy   *It's a Wonderful Life!*

Martin   Hardly.

Billy   Take it up to him. Go on.

Leo *and* **Paulina**.

Leo   Does it matter that I still love you?

Paulina   Sadly. No.

Leo   That I need you.

Paulina   Sorry.

Billy *and* **Martin**.

Billy   I won the crème de menthe.
Have it.
It goes with your jacket.

Martin   Can we go now?

Billy   If you want.

10

Darkness. The sound of traffic passing on a motorway. **Dorothy**
hitching. No lorry stops. She clutches herself.

11

Sunset. **Leo**, *holding his car keys, is standing on the balcony of an Eden
Court block.* **Sheena** *next to him.*

Sheena   You can see your new site, from here.
I've watched it. Watched the cranes pull it all up.
Watched the wrecking ball.
It looks pretty from a distance. The docks and everything.
The water in the background. It's pretty.
It looks nice with the sunset.
When I first lived here I watched the ships.
Watched the men loading and unloading.

Cars and crates of whisky, loads of coal and sacks of bananas.
I thought it was a privilege. Living above the docks.
Watching over the city's front door. And then the front door closed.
Containers.
You know the containers you put on ships, on lorries . . .
As soon as they invented containers there was no need for docks in the city centre. No need for dockers. A port and a motorway's all you need. The crane lifts the box out of the ship and onto the back of the truck. Done.
So the dockers and the sailors lost their jobs and you got yours . . . making museums and restaurants out of warehouses and whisky bonds.
Even the tarts moved inland.
All that got left here was people who were stuck.
Stuck in boxes on the dockside waiting to be picked up.
Hoping someone's going to stop for us and take us with them.

12

The roof of a tall building. Sunset. **Billy** *and* **Martin**. **Billy** *is drinking crème de menthe.*

Billy   Just exactly what is it that you want to do?
We wanna be free.
We wanna do what we wanna do.
And we wanna get loaded.
And we wanna have a good time.

Billy *mimes air guitar.* **Billy** *moves to touch* **Martin**. **Martin** *turns him away.*

Martin   Stand still.

Billy   I want to touch you.

Martin   You can't.

Billy   I want to.

Martin   Stop talking.

A pause. **Martin** *unbuckles* **Billy**'s *belt and pulls his jeans down. Still standing behind him, he looks at* **Billy**.

Martin   Pull your shirt over your head.

Billy *does this. He is about to take the T-shirt completely off when* **Martin** *stops him.*

Martin   Leave it there. Keep your hands there. Keep your face covered.

Billy *stands still.* **Martin** *finally moves towards* **Billy** *and embraces him. Still from behind. Wanking him off.*

13

Leo *and* **Sheena** *on the balcony of Eden Court.*

Leo   Have you a family, Sheena?

Sheena   I have a son.

Leo   Grown up?

Sheena   He's dead. Same age as yours. Elliot. He was named after Elliot Gould. Does that make you laugh?

Leo   No.

Sheena   It makes me laugh. Makes me cringe to think about it.

Leo   How did he die?

Sheena   He stepped off the balcony.
I was in the kitchen. He was watching telly.
I came through and he wasn't there.
I thought he'd gone out.
They didn't know who he was when they found him.
They had to knock on all the doors in the block to see who was missing.
He was depressed. If you're depressed and there's a high

balcony, apparently it's a red rag to a bull.

Leo   I'm sorry.

Sheena   Not your fault. He was depressed.

Leo   This place'd be enough to depress anybody.

Sheena   He was depressed. Elliot wasn't special. People jump here all the time. That's the trouble with architects. You think you're responsible for everything. You think it's all under your doing. You don't think this campaign's about Elliot, do you?

Leo   I don't know. Is it?

Sheena   You're not God, Mr Black. You're an architect. God's a different campaign altogether. This is about housing It's about people having an effect.

Leo   A destructive effect.

Sheena   Maybe.

Leo   They've blown up others. They blew up one in Glasgow and they're blowing them up in Hackney. I don't suppose anyone'll miss this place. I don't even know if I will.

Sheena   Why did you come here, Mr Black?

Leo   To talk to you.

Sheena   What did you want to say?

Leo   I just wanted to explain . . . the idea . . . the dream behind this mess. It was a good . . . It wasn't malicious.

Sheena   You wanted me to tell you you were a nice man.

Leo   No . . .
Yes.

Sheena   It doesn't matter. Whether you're a nice man or not doesn't matter.

Leo   It does to me.

Sheena   I can't help you with that.

Leo The new place, if they build it, it'll be exactly the same, you know.

Sheena I'm not stupid. I'm not a silly wee woman who doesn't like modern buildings. You're right. I know this is 'good design'. 'Good design' isn't the point. The point is control. Who has the power to knock down and who has the power to build.

Leo Even if it's wrong.

Sheena Even if it's wrong.

14

Billy, *alone, walking along the edge of the roof, drinking crème de menthe.*

Darkness.

15

Leo, **Paulina** *and* **Dorothy** *having a meal. Silence.* **Martin** *enters.*

Martin Any for me, Boss? I'm famished.

Leo Sit down, Martin.

Martin Oh. It's one of those.

Dorothy Just sit down, will you?

Martin The old family talk.

Leo There's something you ought to know.

Martin Fire away.

Leo Your mother and I . . .

Paulina Your father's leaving.

Martin Oh.

Leo   Temporarily. We've decided. There's been, a tension, I'm sure you've noticed.

Martin   What do you want me to say?

Leo   This doesn't affect you, of course, this is still your home . . .

Martin   Am I supposed to say something?

Paulina   Say what you want to say.

Dorothy   Does anybody want any water?

Leo   If you want to talk about it. Of course we can talk about it.
Do you? Do you want to talk about it?

Martin   . . .
No.

Dorothy   Anyone? Water?

Leo   We'll still be a family, of course. Obviously we still . . . both of us . . . still love –

Martin   What about money?

Dorothy   Martin.

Martin   I'm sorry. I didn't mean to say that. I meant . . .

Leo   I don't think you need to worry about money.

Martin   Sorry.

Silence.

What are you going to do?

Paulina   What do you mean?

Martin   Now. What are you going to do. Take up singing? Hang-glide? Take a lover? Fulfil those buried dreams?

Paulina   Don't be crass.

Martin   What then?

Dorothy   If you don't mind I'll . . .

Paulina   Nothing in particular.

Dorothy   I'd like to go now. If you want me to stay I can
stay . . .

Martin   Nothing in particular. All this for nothing in
particular.

Dorothy   If there's anything I can do.
Is there?

Martin   Seems a bit drastic.

Dorothy   There's nothing I can do. So if you don't mind I'll
go out for a while.

Paulina   You don't have to go.

Dorothy   I do.

Martin   Me too, in fact . . . said I'd be somewhere.

Leo   We need to talk about the future.

Martin   Who gets what?

Leo   The future, Martin.

Martin   Oh. I'd rather . . .
I don't know the way to speak in these situations.
Do you?
I'll only say the wrong thing again. Have the wrong idea.
I'd rather leave you to it.

Dorothy *and* **Martin** *leave.*

Leo   Martin!

Paulina   Leave them.

Leo   We can't just –

Paulina   Leave them.

16

The roof. **Martin** *wearing the green jacket carrying a small rucksack. An empty bottle of crème de menthe. The sound of an ambulance below.*

Martin   Billy?
Billy?
Where are you?
Billy . . .
Let's go . . .
We're going to Fife, Billy.
Billy?
Fuck.

Darkness.

17

Leo *with the model of Eden Court.* **Paulina** *near him.*

Leo   In the past we built cities on top of cities . . .
in the middle of cities . . .
around them . . .
Haphazard, unplanned . . . encrustations.
Layers of mistakes corrected by more mistakes . . .
Never a clean slate.
Never a clear vision.
So when they asked me to build something I thought . . .
Duty required me to . . .
I thought I had to make . . .
Because of the future . . .
A new idea. A better thing.
Look.
A thousand families . . . self-contained flats . . . connecting
walkways . . . public galleries and . . . space and . . .
structure and . . .
And the stones . . . each block represents a stone, a
monolith . . .
Do you see? Timeless.

A family in each flat.
Each block a community.
The whole estate a village.
The city encircled by estates, each one connected to the others
and to the centre.
Everything connected to the centre.
Do you see?
A design.
But it's the human element, isn't it?
Materials, structure and so on . . . but the human
element . . .
Eludes you.
You can't design for it.

Paulina   Maybe they'll ask you to build the new ones.

Leo   I don't think so.

Paulina   Maybe you and Martin.
It could be a project for you.

Leo   Maybe.

Paulina   You could offer. Put in a plan.

Leo   No point in a plan.

Paulina   Why not?

Leo   No point in planning if anything you build can be
turned into a prison.

Paulina   Houses though, Leo.

Leo   Anything you think up can be made dangerous.

Paulina   Still. You and Martin. You could teach him. Talk
to him. Make progress.

Leo   No matter how high you build something. No matter
how well you build it. No matter how beautiful it is. You can't
build a thing high enough that if you fell off you wouldn't hit
the ground.

18

A morgue. **Martin** *sitting next to* **Billy**'s *body.* **Dorothy** *comes in.*

Dorothy   Who is he?

Martin   A friend. An acquaintance. He had my name in his pocket. That's all.

Dorothy   When you phoned . . . you sounded like you wanted someone.

Martin   Did I? I've been trying all my life to sound like that. Never managed before.

Dorothy   Is he a . . . did you . . . ?

Martin   We fucked a few times.

Dorothy   I'm sorry.

Martin   He ran off the roof of a block of flats.
Spoiled his looks apart from anything else.
His body sort of burst. He spoiled himself.
You don't get the right impression seeing him like this.

Dorothy   Do you know why he did it?

Martin   I was going to leave and he wanted to come with me. I wouldn't let him.

Dorothy   It's not your fault, Martin.

Martin   I know.

Dorothy   You mustn't feel it's your fault.

Martin   I don't.

Dorothy   Do his family know yet?

Martin   No.

Dorothy   Will you tell them?

Martin   I don't know who they are. Don't even know if he's got one. I never asked. Someone else'll tell them. There must be someone who's job it is to tell people that kind of thing.

Dorothy *goes over to hold* **Martin**.

Martin   Don't. It makes me feel uncomfortable.

Dorothy   Sorry.

Martin *touches* **Billy**'s *face. Gingerly.*

Dorothy   Do you want me to leave?

Martin   No. Stay.

Dorothy   I don't know what to say.

Martin   What effect do you want?

Dorothy   Sorry?

Martin   You want to say the right thing. What effect would saying the right thing achieve?

Dorothy   I want to comfort you.

Martin   Don't say anything then. I'll try and feel that anyway. Save you searching for words.

Dorothy   He was young.

Martin   I've never seen a dead body before. I've dreamt of it. I've thought about what it would be like. I've imagined myself dead. Everyone crowded round me. Tears etc. I've imagined you dead. Never seen it though. It's not as dramatic as I thought. It's not as beautiful. It's just Billy's empty.

Dorothy   Maybe he's in a better place. Happy somewhere.

Martin   What an ugly thought.

Dorothy   I only meant . . . we don't know.

Martin   The interesting thing is. Looking at him. Now. Me beside him. You here watching. I feel. Quite happy in a way. I feel powerful. It's almost erotic. As though for the first time I'm entitled to be . . . anything. I'm entitled to say . . . anything. To do anything. I could make a pass at you, or spit at you, or weep and you wouldn't ask me to explain, I'd be entitled.

Dorothy   Maybe.

Martin   What do you fucking mean maybe. Of course I fucking could. You'd do anything for me. You fucking worship me. You came here, didn't you? I told you to and you came, didn't you?

Dorothy   Yes.

Martin   See.
You've got that look on your face.
Tolerance.
Awe.
Fear.
When I came to the reception the woman looked at me.
She gave me that look.
I want everyone to look at me that way.
Always.
Maybe I'll have to kill you next.

Dorothy   We should leave. We're not his real family. We shouldn't be here.

Martin   You go. I want to stay.

Dorothy   Will you be long?

Martin   I don't think I ever want to move.

Dorothy *leaves.* **Martin** *looks at* **Billy** *for a while. He kisses* **Billy**. *Holds him.*

Martin   Fuck. Fuck. Fuck. Fuck.

Darkness.

19

Leo *and* **Sheena**, *in* **Leo**'s *office, studying blueprints.*

Sheena   I came to say thank ypu.

Leo   No need.

Sheena   I wanted to.

Leo   Where have they moved you to?

Sheena   Temporary places. Near the motorway.

Leo   Very nice.

Sheena   I've been working on the new designs.
It's a woman, the person we're working with.
You maybe know her. She does community architecture.

Leo   Probably not.

Sheena   She's very good. Helpful . . .

Lee   I'm glad.

Sheena   What are you doing?

Leo   The demolition people need blueprints so the
explosives can be placed correctly. At the points of weakness.
They need to know where the weaknesses are so they can
design the explosion. They want the structure to fall in on
itself.

Sheena   And you know where the weaknesses are?

Leo   I thought so.

Sheena   I just thought you'd put a bomb under it.

Leo   It's a complex job destroying buildings as big as this.
You can't just watch it topple. It's more clinical than that,
more surgical. The taller the building the more you need to
control it, or else the whole thing falls sideways, takes other
buildings with it, falls into the crowd. It's an interesting
operation.

Sheena   Will you be there? On the day?

Leo   Maybe.

Sheena   There'll be quite a crowd.

Leo   People love to watch things fall. The bigger the better.

Sheena   One of the kids from the estate won the
competition to press the detonator.

Leo   It's not a real detonator, you know.

Sheena   Really?

Leo   Just for show. Engineers control the process. It's all computerised nowadays. The kid's just there for the cameras.

Sheena   I hope nobody tells him. It'd be like telling him Santa Claus doesn't exist.

Leo   Do you still have a set of keys, Ms Mackie?

Sheena   Keys?

Leo   For your flat.

Sheena   I think so. Why?

Leo   I'd like to borrow them.

Sheena   What for?

Leo   Last look around. Take some photos. Nostalgia. Keep a record of them before they go.

Sheena   If you want. I don't need them.

She gives him a set of keys.

Leo   Thank you.

Sheena   You know, I fancy this job, Mr Black.
Do you think you can do courses?
At my age?

Leo   I'm sure you can.

Sheena   Now the campaign's finished I'm fired up for something new . . . You know. I feel . . . Do you think I'd be any good?

Leo   You've got strong ideas.

Sheena   I'd really like to do it.

Leo   You should.

Sheena   Maybe I could work for you.

Leo   I'd be happy to have you.

Sheena   That's nice of you to say.

Leo   I mean it.

Sheena   Well. I came to say thank you for what you've done.

Leo   Don't mention it.

Sheena   I know my way out.

Leo   Good luck. Ms Mackie.

20

Dorothy *and* **Joe** *in the cab of* **Joe***'s lorry.*

Dorothy   Where are we going this time?

Joe   Glasgow.

Dorothy   What's Glasgow like?

Joe   Violent.

Dorothy   I thought Glaswegians were supposed to be friendly.

Joe   Violent but friendly. That's supposed to be the characteristic.

Dorothy   Maybe I should stay there.

Joe   Running away again?

Dorothy   I missed you. I waited for you at the side of the road but you never stopped.

Joe   I must have missed you too. Didn't see you or something. I had my eyes straight ahead. I don't often look for hitchers, you get hypnotised by the road.

Dorothy   I tried sending you dolphin calls. You mustn't have picked them up.

Joe   Maybe I did. I stopped this time.

Dorothy   What's in the back?

Joe   Who knows? It's a container. I pick up the box from the boat. Could be anything. Machinery. Grain. Meat. Metal. Anything. Could be empty.

Dorothy   You're a nice man, Joe.

Joe   Don't say that.

Dorothy   Why not? You are.

Joe   You don't know anything about me.

Dorothy   I don't need to. I can tell.

Joe   I could be a killer. Or a rapist. Maybe I pick up women and rape them in the back of the truck. Other drivers do.

Dorothy   Do you?

Joe   No.

Dorothy   Have you thought about it?

Joe   Yes.

Dorothy   You wouldn't.

Joe   That's what I say.

Dorothy   Did you miss me?

Joe   A little.

Dorothy   Do you love me?

Joe   No.

Dorothy   Could you love me?

Joe   I'll take you anywhere you want to go. I'll do anything you want me to do. I'll talk to you all night. That's better than love. You don't want me to love you.

Dorothy   How do you know?

Joe   If I loved you I'd hurt you.

Dorothy   You're a nice man, Joe.

21

The sound of dripping water. Agents' public toilet. **Martin** *stands in a urinal, a Jenners' bag next to him.*

22

Dorothy *and* **Joe** *in the truck.*

23

Paulina *potting plants.*

24

Leo *opens the door to an empty flat.*

A siren.

A voice speaks through a loud hailer.

Voice   STAND CLEAR!
STAND CLEAR!
STAND CLEAR PLEASE.
STAND WELL BACK.

The siren sounds a second time.

Leo *is alone. He looks out of the window. The sound of a crowd chanting 'ten, nine, eight, seven, six, five, four, three, two, one . . . ' There is a moment of stillness.*

Darkness.

The sound of a series of explosions.

The sound of a crowd cheering and clapping.

The cosmonaut's last message to the woman he once loved in the former Soviet Union

The cosmonaut's last message to the woman he once loved in the former Soviet Union was first performed by Paines Plough at the Ustinov Studio, Theatre Royal, Bath, on 15 April 1999. The cast was as follows:

Keith/Bernard	Kenneth Bryans
Vivienne/Sylvia	Morag Hood
Oleg/Patient	Rob Jarvis
Nastasja/Claire	Danièle Lydon
Eric/Proprietors	Neil McKinven
Casimir/Patient	Andy Smart

Directed by Vicky Featherstone
Designed by Georgia Sion
Lighting by Nigel J. Edwards
Music and sound by Nick Powell

My grateful thanks to the following people and institutions who gave me support and advice during the writing of this play: Suspect Culture, Irina Brown and the Tron Theatre, Vicki Featherstone and Paines Plough, the Traverse Theatre, all the actors involved in the TRON and RSAMD workshops, Alan Wilkins, and as always Lucie and Annie.

for Jill and David and Mel . . .

. . . Space dark I see.
Is my men last. Men are that first.
That moon is there. They have some dust.
Is home they know. Blue earth I think.
I lift I see. It is that command.
My men go back. I leave that there.
It is bright so.

Edwin Morgan – 'Thoughts of a Module'

Characters

Oleg, *a cosmonaut.*
Casimir, *a cosmonaut.*
Keith, *a civil servant.*
Vivienne, *a speech therapist.*
Nastasja, *an erotic dancer.*
Eric, *an official of the World Bank.*
Claire, *a policewoman.*
Bernard, *a UFO researcher.*
Patient, *a man or woman who has had a stroke.*
Sylvia, *an erotic dancer.*
Proprietors, *the owners of bars.*

Actors

Actor 1 (Keith, Bernard), *a man in his early fifties.*
Actor 2 (Proprietors, Eric), *a man in his thirties.*
Actor 3 (Patient), *a man or woman in their seventies.*
Actor 4 (Oleg), *a man in his forties.*
Actor 5 (Casimir), *a man in his forties.*
Actress 1 (Vivienne, Sylvia), *a woman in her forties.*
Actress 2 (Nastasja, Claire), *a woman in her early twenties.*

Setting

Recently.

Act One

1

Darkness.
Stars appear.
One star is moving, describing an arc across the night sky.
A sad song from a Soviet choir.

Oleg *and* **Casimir** *on board the Harmony 114 module.* **Oleg** *is floating, absorbed in the music.* **Casimir** *is fixing the radio.* **Oleg** *has to shout over the music.*

Oleg   They've forgotten us.

Casimir   What?

Oleg   They've forgotten us.

Casimir   I can't hear you.

Oleg   They have forgotten us.

Casimir   I've done it.

Oleg   What?

Casimir *flicks a switch.*
White noise.

2

A summer evening.

Keith *and* **Vivienne** *in a comfortable middle-class home in Edinburgh. The large shutters over the windows are closed.* **Keith** *sits on a large sofa.* **Vivienne** *sits on another large sofa. The television is not working. Showing static.*

A pause.

Vivienne   What happened?

Keith   It'll be a fault.

Vivienne   Have we paid all our bills?

Keith   I think I can fix it.
It's probably just the aerial.

He tries, and is unable, to fix it.

Vivienne   Maybe there's been a mix-up.
With the computers.
So they think we're behind on payment.

Keith   Could be. Is there a wind? It's quiet.

Vivienne   Why did it just go off suddenly? There wasn't any
warning.

Keith   It'll be a fault. Possibly a transmitter fault. Could be
our aerial. It could be some type of power surge across the
grid that's blown something in a sub-station somewhere.

Vivienne   . . .

Keith   There'll be a message soon. It'll come to life again
and they'll apologise for the fault.

Keith *sits back down.*
A pause.
They look at the screen.

Keith   All we can do is wait.

Vivienne *looks at* **Keith**.

Vivienne   We could go for a walk.

Keith   A walk?

Vivienne   We could . . .

Keith   It's too late. It's dark. It's cold.

Vivienne   It's not cold. It's warm. It's hot. We could –

Keith   It's warm inside. The central heating. It's too high.
I'm sweating like a pig.

Vivienne   You're probably right.

Keith   It'll be fixed in a minute. Wait a minute.

He gets down on the floor in front of the TV. He examines the screen closely.

I can see something.

He gets up. He groans at the effort of getting up.

Something's about to happen.

Vivienne   You know, for a second then –

Keith   It looked like we were getting something.

Vivienne   Yes.

Keith   Something seemed to be coming through.

Vivienne   For a second, just then . . .

Keith   But I lost it.

Vivienne   When you did that. What you just did.

Keith   What did I do?

Vivienne   You know. You . . . the way you groaned when you got up from the floor.

Keith   I groaned?

Vivienne   I could see your father.

Keith   Oh right.

Vivienne   When he would get up from his chair.
Remember. When we used to sit on the sofa in your house.
In that house. Eating biscuits. (*Groans.*) 'I'll just have a biscuit.'

Keith   I remember.

Vivienne (*groans*)   'I'll just have a biscuit.'

Keith   We'll probably have nothing for a moment or two.
Until it's fixed.

Vivienne   He leant forward just like you did then. 'I'll just have a biscuit.'

Keith   We'll just have to sit it out . . .

Vivienne   And your mum . . .

A look.

We could have a drink. Have we got some? Something . . .
some . . .

Keith   Do you want a drink?

Vivienne   Maybe . . . but if you're not. I won't.

Keith   Go ahead. I don't mind.

Vivienne   No.

Keith   Should we switch the television off?

Vivienne   Leave it.
We'll see if something happens.

Keith   OK.
I'm sweating like a pig.
The effort.

He takes off his tie. He lays it on the sofa beside him.
Something of a pause.

Vivienne   I looked at the sky this evening.

Keith   Really?

Vivienne   Red sky at night. Shepherd's delight.

Keith   Happy shepherds then.

Vivienne   You do get such beautiful skies in this city. I
thought once, the houses here have such high ceilings and the
sky always seems so . . . high.

Keith   Apparently it's dust in the atmosphere.
The particles of matter . . . refract.
That causes the redness.

Vivienne   Oh.

Keith   When you think about it.
It might be what's wrong with the telly.

Vivienne   I think I might go and get a drink.
Are you sure you don't want one.

Keith   Please. A small one.

She leaves the room.
He tries to make the TV work.
It flickers into life.
News.

3

On the Harmony 114 module.

Casimir   Hello? Hello? Is anybody listening?
This is Soviet Special Orbital Craft Harmony 114.
My name is Dr Casimir . . .

Oleg *pulls a chunk of wires from a socket.*

Casimir   No! Oleg!
Hello?
Hello?

4

In the living-room.

The TV has gone back to static.

Keith   Shit.

Vivienne *re-enters with two large whiskies.*

Vivienne   Sometimes I think we should get rid of it.
Throw it out.
Smash it.
Or . . . put it in a cupboard.
And read.
Maybe I would read if it went.
Or listen to some sort of music.

Keith   Shh!

Vivienne   What?

Keith   I thought I heard something. Some noise.

Vivienne   Where?

Keith   Outside.
I thought maybe there might be someone . . .

She goes to the shutters. Listens.

Vivienne   I can't hear anything.

Keith   It's probably nothing.

Vivienne   It's probably just the wind.

Keith   Only with the television. It could be . . . kids . . . I thought. Fiddling with the aerial.

Vivienne   Maybe.

Keith   I've noticed. The new houses. They have kids, they mooch around.

Vivienne   We should never have sold the land.

Keith   Maybe it's a prank.

Vivienne   Just in a few years. All those flats suddenly spring up.

Keith   Some kids taking the piss.

Vivienne   All that space. That lovely wild garden.

Keith   You don't like gardens.

Vivienne   I would have liked the chance to . . . design a garden.

Keith   We didn't need a garden.

Vivienne   I'm just saying there's a difference between a wild garden and then . . . a block of flats just springs up.

Keith   Maybe I should go out and see . . .

Vivienne   I doubt it's anything. A cat maybe.

Keith   They're probably nice kids.
That's the awful thing.

Vivienne   There was that man. I worry about you
sometimes. That man who went out one evening and they just
cut his throat. The local kids . . . His son was standing in the
doorway.

Keith   I don't think . . .

Vivienne   I know. I'm just being . . .

Keith   I wish you wouldn't read about these things.

Vivienne   I know.

Keith   Because statistically.

Vivienne   His son.

Keith   It isn't . . .

Vivienne   Poor boy.

Keith   I don't think I'll bother going out.

Vivienne   No.

Something of a pause.

Vivienne   You'd think they could print some joy.
Tell us something . . . joyful.
Sometimes.
I know it's stupid. I know . . .

Keith   I agree with you.

Vivienne   Because it's news and one should know the truth
about things.
But there must be some . . .
Joy.

Keith   We should have got cable.

Vivienne   Cable?

Keith   When the man came and offered it.

Vivienne   Oh yes.

Keith   Because the reception . . . it goes underground . . . it's reliable.

Vivienne   Not through the sky.

Keith   No.

Vivienne   It's hardly joy though, is it?
All that pornography.
I'd rather read
I'd rather we got rid of it.
Put it in a cupboard and we could read.

Keith   I'm sweating like a pig. Are you sure the heating's not . . . ?

Vivienne   Sure.

Keith   OK.

They look at the screen. **Keith** *fiddles with the tie. He opens up the shirt collar. He puts the tie into the collar. He is tying it loosely.*

I bought a new tie.
Just thought I'd liven myself up.

He shows her the design.

Vivienne   Can I see it?

He gives it to her. She examines it. She reads the label on the back.

Mont Saint Victoire.
By Paul Cézanne.

Keith   They do a lot of them.

Vivienne   It's nice.

Keith   A few different painters.
Mainly impressionists.
And abstract.

Vivienne   The things you get.
One gets.

Keith   I just thought I needed. Livening up.

Something of a pause.

I'm actually damp.
With sweat.

Vivienne   We could open the shutters.

Keith   Let some air in.

Vivienne   Open the window a little.

Keith   See if those kids are mooching about.
. . .
I haven't heard anything.
Maybe they're waiting.
Listening in.

He stands in front of the shutters just long enough for us to see that he is very afraid.

GO ON PISS OFF!
. . .
PISS OFF!

Vivienne *stands.*

Keith   They're probably just playing.

Keith *listens.*
He opens the shutters.
The windows are tall and elegant. The night sky starlit. Light transparent curtains.

Vivienne   Open the window.

He heaves the windows. They open a little. A breeze. They stand together.

Stars.

Keith   You forget.
You forget what's up there.

Vivienne   There's a plant smell . . . I can . . . on the breeze.

Keith   Is that what it is?

Vivienne   It's mint . . . or . . . is it mint?

Keith   Someone from the flats must have planted it.

Vivienne   I had no idea.

Keith   No sign of those kids.

Vivienne   No.

Keith   It's going to be hot again tomorrow.

Vivienne   We should do something.
Let's do something together.

Keith   I have to go to London.
I hate travelling on hot days.
You feel like a crated animal.
. . .

Vivienne   I might sit outdoors and read a book or something.

She puts her arm around his waist.

5

On board the Harmony 114.

Casimir   I had established communication. You fuck.
I had.
Fuck. Fuck. Cuh . . . Fuh . . .
Fixed.
You fucking military fuck.
The communications.

Oleg   Casimir. I am a fellow officer. I am your senior officer.

Casimir   You cuh . . .

Oleg   Please don't speak to me with that tone.

Casimir   The rage I . . .

Oleg   If there's something you want to say to me –

Casimir   Fuh . . . fuh . . . God.

A pause. **Casimir** *can find no words, no vocalisation with which to encapsulate his emotion.*

Oleg   – please feel free to record your comments in the log.

Casimir *launches an attack on* **Oleg**. **Oleg** *is too fit. Too strong.*

Casimir   Smash your fucking face.
Smash your face into your fucking brain.
I'll strangle you.
Strangle you.
Please, God. Kind God.
Lovely God, I beg You
Give me the strength to strangle this cunt spaceman.
God is my friend, Oleg. I warn you.
I can feel it.
I warn you.
I can feel lovely God pumping strength back into my
knuckles.
LORD OF THE UNIVERSE.
If You give me only enough strength for one last act.
Let it be to cause his death.
I beg You.

Casimir *collapses. The energy of his attack on* **Oleg** *has worn him out.* **Oleg** *embraces* **Casimir**. *He finds a bottle of oxygen and lifts the mask to* **Casimir***'s mouth.* **Casimir** *is dangerously weak.*

Oleg   This is the mission, comrade.
Let me give you strength.
We're trained.

He manoeuvres **Casimir** *to a screen. The screen comes to life. A colour image of earth.*

Siberia, Casimir.
Look.
Baikal.
No clouds.
Your daughter standing on the shore. Sending messages to her daddy. Your lovely daughter on the lakeside.

What colour is her hair?

Casimir   I don't know.

Oleg   Her eyes.

Casimir   I don't remember any more.

Oleg   Every day we pass over Baikal and every day she looks up.
Every day, Casimir.
She calls out to you.

Casimir   Cool water.

Oleg   Think of the water in the lake.

Casimir   Can't remember.

Oleg   Try.

Casimir   I can't.

Oleg   Remember cool water.

Casimir   I don't want to *remember* cool water, you cunt. I want to swim in it.

Oleg   She's swimming. In the cool water. No clouds over the lake.
Nastasja's swimming. I can see her.

Casimir   I don't know what she looks like.

Oleg   Dark hair. Her eyes . . . calling for you.

Casimir   Please, God, he's torturing me.
Make it stop.
Make it stop.

6

A café in Heathrow airport.

The sound of a jet aircraft taking off and landing. **Nastasja** *is sitting on a stool. The* **Proprietor** *is nearby. She watches him work. He notices.*

Proprietor   I speak six languages, you know.
What are you?
You French?
You German?
You a Yank?
You Spanish?
You Brazilian?
. . .
. . .
You a tart? You looking for business? I'm interested.

She reacts, offended.
. . .
Sorry.
Do you want a cappuccino? I'll give it you for nothing.
To say sorry.
I was totally out of order there.
I dunno what came over me.
I've got a daughter your age.
You a long way from home?
You look it. You look lost.
They'll eat you up out there.
Take my advice.
Don't accept anything.
Tell them to fuck off.
If you're foreign they'll take advantage.
You're all right in the airport.
But out there . . .
They'll tear you apart. Pretty thing like you.
Go on.
Have a cappuccino. On me.

He's made the coffee. He makes a show of turning it round and giving it to her with a flourish.

Ta da!

She smiles.

Nastasja   Thank you.

Proprietor   There you go.

You've got a pretty smile.
You should be in films.
You'd wipe the floor with them.
What's your name?

Nastasja   Nastasja.

Proprietor   You waiting on a plane, Nastasja?

Nastasja   No.

Proprietor   Just arrived, have you?

Nastasja   I'm waiting for a person.

Proprietor   You be careful.

Nastasja   Why?

Proprietor   I know. I'm telling you. I see all kinds. All kinds from all over the world. And I'm telling you. You've got a lovely smile. Don't let them spoil it. Eh? You got a husband?

Nastasja   No.

Proprietor   You got a daddy?

Nastasja   He's up there.
In the stars.
He went there when I was only six years old.
I still talk to him.

Proprietor   You have to accept death, love.
Hard as it may be.
We're all mortal.
I can't sleep at night thinking about what my little girl'll do when I go. Poor little puppy. I love her something rotten. But she'll have to go on without me. She'll just have to go on.

Keith *enters. Walks up to* **Nastasja**. *They kiss.*

Keith   The plane was delayed. Weather. Some electrical storm over Nottingham or something. My shirt's sticking to my back. I'm sweating like a pig.

Nastasja   Not – ingm.
So many places in England.

Keith (*to* **Proprietor**)   Cappuccino.
At one stage I thought we were going down.
It was terrifying.
And then the pilot was a woman.
A woman's voice saying 'we're experiencing a little
turbulence'.
I'm still shaking.

Nastasja   I love storms.

Keith   I know.

Nastasja   So many places in England.

Keith   I'm just a bit shaken.
The pilot being a woman.
I don't know why.

He embraces her. Kisses her.

Nastasja   Big black clouds over a lake.
Standing in the face of the wind.
Falling forward.
Poor Keith.
I should have been with you.
I could have held you.

They begin to leave.

Proprietor   You be careful.
Your daddy's in heaven.
He's watching over you.
You look after yourself.

Nastasja   I will, mister.

Proprietor   You make sure.

7

On board the Harmony 114.

Oleg *is exercising.* **Casimir** *is shuffling playing cards. On the back of the cards are pictures of naked women.*

Casimir Anna.
Collette.
Eva.
Lily.
I've slept with every one of these.
I want new cards.

Oleg   Every one?

Casimir Every one. In a thousand different ways. Each way a thousand times.

Oleg   I've rationed myself. I chose one card. Vanessa. At first it was good . . . then I looked at some of the other cards and I thought . . . 'Maybe I shouldn't ration. Maybe I should explore all the women first and see which one is the best.' But then . . .
I fell in love with Vanessa.
I took time to imagine clearly every single part of her body. The smells of her body. The tastes of her body. The tiniest blemish on the skin of her thigh. The scar on her forehead where she was injured by a tree when she was riding through the forest.
It was a very loving time for us.
But after a while it became . . .
(*He searches for a word.*)
I was numb.
I hated her.
Then . . . I realised how deeply I loved her.
Now she's boring me again.

Casimir   I've slept with all of these women except Vanessa and Katia.

Oleg   You haven't slept with Vanessa?

Casimir   How can I? You keep the card in your pocket. It's worn through. The card's deteriorated from the sweat of your fingers. I can barely make out an image. She's useless.

Oleg   I want you to sleep with Vanessa.
It would add spice.
It might help . . . rekindle my feelings for her.

Casimir   I have no interest in Vanessa.

Oleg   What about Katia? Why don't you sleep with Katia?

Casimir   I can't.

Oleg   Why not?

Casimir   Katia is my daughter.

Oleg   No?

Casimir   Years ago. The first time you asked me what colour her eyes were, what colour her hair was . . . I realised I couldn't picture them anymore. So I used Katia's eyes. Then when I couldn't picture her face I used Katia's face . . . and so on . . . until now.

Oleg   You must remember your daughter.
I don't believe you.

Casimir   No.

Oleg   Fifty is still plenty of women.

Casimir   I want to sleep with Katia now.

Oleg   You shouldn't.

Casimir   I'm going to do it.

Oleg   Don't.

Casimir   Why not?
Who is she, anyway?
Just some woman.

Oleg   You're upset. Talk to me . . .

Casimir   I'm going. Right now.

Oleg COMRADE!
I order you . . .
In the name of the peoples of the Union of Soviet Socialist
Republics.
Give me the card.
. . .
Save her.
Give her to me.
. . .
. . .
I'll sleep with her.
Take her to a little hotel, away from my wife. Make love in the
afternoon.
. . .
With your permission of course.

Casimir *gives him the card.*

Casimir *laughs then* **Oleg** *laughs as well.*

8

A hotel room in London.

Keith *is dressing in his suit and tie. The large windows are open on to a*
balcony. **Nastasja***, half undressed, gets out of bed, takes a beer from the*
minibar and goes out to the balcony to drink it. **Keith** *shuts the minibar*
door.

Nastasja   It's beautiful. You take me to the best fucking
shitty places. Can I stay the night here? Look at these small
houses. Hardly any tall buildings anywhere. Look at the trees.
Houses and trees going all the way to the sea. Come out here
and feel the breeze on your skin.

Keith   Do you want some money?

Nastasja   Don't talk about that. Come and stand with me.

Keith   How much do you need?

Nastasja   GOOD AFTERNOON MR LONDON!

How are you?
I am fine thank you, how are you?
I am fine. How are you?
I am fine. How are you?

Keith *leaves some money on the bedside table.*
He puts his jacket on.
He takes his jacket off.
Nastasja *comes back in and flops on to the bed.*

Nastasja   Will you take me to dinner tonight?

Keith   I can't . . . I'm sorry.

Nastasja   We'll come back here together.

Keith   I have to go home.

Nastasja   You don't have to.

Keith   I have to.

Nastasja   It's OK. You'll come back.

Keith   Why are you so happy today?

Nastasja   Why are you not?

Keith   Because I . . .
I . . .
I'm unhappy because I have to leave you.

Nastasja   Don't say fucking shit.

Keith   Sorry.

Nastasja   Don't say fucking lies to me. I'm not English.

Keith   Neither am I.

Nastasja   Take me to dinner tonight. To some extra special place.

Keith   I'd like to do that.
Next time.
I'll take you somewhere special.

Nastasja   Where?

Keith   Somewhere in Scotland.
I'll take you to the mountains.
Skye.
It's beautiful, there's . . .
If it doesn't rain.
It's famous.

Nastasja   Sky is always beautiful. I like storms.

Keith   It's an island.

Nastasja   An island called sky.

Keith   I should go.

Nastasja   Where do film people go in London?

Keith   I don't know.

Nastasja   Everyone knows where film people go in cities.

Keith   I don't.
I know where civil servants go.

Nastasja   Stop talking fuck shit.

Keith   I'm not.

Nastasja   I want to be discovered in a film.
I'm more beautiful.

Keith   You are.

Nastasja   Don't tell me. I can see for myself.
I'm the best dancer.
And I can act too.

Keith   It's a difficult world to get into . . .

Nastasja   Let's have children.

Keith   . . .

Nastasja   I love children. Would you like to have children with me? You would be such a good father.

Keith   Can we not –

Nastasja   Playing with children all over the floor.

Keith   – talk about this please, Nastasja.

Nastasja   And I'll come in from filming. I'll be tired. Here's little Alexei . . . come to me, Alexei.

Keith   Don't talk about this.

Nastasja   Don't talk.
I'm not fucking English with shit.

Keith   I know.
I'm sorry.

Nastasja   You stop. Stop me talking. Shut me up.

Keith   I know. It's . . . habit. I . . .

Nastasja   My father was a cosmonaut.
He left to go into space when I was six.
He said, Nastasja, whenever you want to talk and you have no one to talk to, stand on the edge of the lake and look up to the sky. I will be looking down. He never came back to earth. I still talk to him.

Keith   Nastasja . . .
I have to tell you something.
I . . .

Nastasja   Take me to dinner.

Keith   I have to go home.

Nastasja   You're a liar.

Keith   It's so hot today.
I hate travelling on hot days.
You feel like a crated animal.
I have to go home.

Nastasja   That's why you're unhappy.

Keith   I can't take you to dinner.

Nastasja   Leave your wife.

Keith   I've told you –

Nastasja   Coward. Liar.
You want to run away.

Keith   I don't. Honestly.
I want to stay with you.
I used to hate London, Nastasja.
I couldn't stand the traffic and the people and the stink.
But since I've met you I . . .
I love this city.
Every street.
Every bridge.
Every underpass.
Every park.
. . .
. . .
. . .
You shouldn't be with me.
I'm like a damp towel over a flame.
. . .
I hate this city.

Nastasja   It's easy to be happy.

Keith   No.

Nastasja   Don't fuck shit.
If you choose unhappy then you choose it.
Don't fuck shit on my account.

Keith   I want to be happy very much.

Nastasja   Will you come back tonight?
Will you take me to dinner?

Keith   Yes.

Nastasja   I'll find out where film people go.

Keith   Nastasja, I . . .

Nastasja   Say.

Keith   I'm embarrassed.

Nastasja   I'm not English.

Keith   Nastasja . . .
I think I'm probably in love with you.
. . .
I . . .
Love you.

Nastasja   I love you.

Keith   How can you possibly?

Nastasja   I can. It's possible.

Keith   . . .

Nastasja *goes out to the balcony.*
Keith *empties his wallet.*
Puts it with the other money on the table.
He leaves.

9

A small patch of cultivated ground in a city.

Vivienne *is holding a packet of seeds. Some herbs are growing. A few flowers. Cars go by very fast on a nearby road.*

Gingerly, **Vivienne** *scratches a hole in the earth. With a pair of nail scissors she opens the seed packet. She pours the seeds into the hole.*

Claire *enters wearing gardening clothes and gloves. She's noticeably but not heavily pregnant.*

Claire   Hello.

Vivienne *is frightened. As if she's been caught.*

Vivienne   Is this yours? Sorry, I . . .

Claire   No.

Vivienne   Are they . . .

Claire   It's yours. It's your ground. But I took the liberty of planting a few . . . well, because, you know you'd never done anything with it and I thought you could always dig them up if they bothered you.

I hate to see things going to waste.

Vivienne   It doesn't bother me. It's . . .

Claire   I'm your neighbour.

Vivienne   Oh. Sorry.

Claire   Claire. I live in the flats.
You might have seen my husband?

Vivienne   I don't know.

Claire   He leaves every morning to drive to work.
A silver Renault.
He's quite big.

Vivienne   There are so many of you I . . .

Claire   It's nice to meet you at last. All the couples in the flats talk about you. We look at your lovely house and we all wonder what it's like inside. You must be very proud of your house. It's so old.

Vivienne   Well . . .

Claire   Gordon's a policeman.
I'm a policewoman. But this little one'll put a stop to that.
I might go back to work when he goes to school.
They won't grow if you do it that way.
You have to plant the seeds one by one.
Throw them all in like that and they fight each other.
I'll do it . . .

She kneels down.
She shows **Vivienne** *how to plant the seeds.*

These herbs are for the little one.
I make herbal teas.
Every disease has a herb that cures it.
I don't like the thought of taking drugs. Even for pain.

Vivienne   I've never given it a thought.

Claire   You should. I can tell you all about it if you want.

Vivienne   Should I pay you?

Claire   What for?

Vivienne   For this. The work?

Claire *is embarrassed.*

Claire   I like doing it.

Vivienne *is embarrassed.*

Claire   And you can always dig it up again.
Gordon and me are going away at the weekend so you might
want to water them yourself

Vivienne   You're going away?

Claire   A trip.
We're going up north. To Skye. Camping.
It's our last chance before the little one.
Skye's the most beautiful place in the world.
And it's in Scotland.
We're so lucky.
Just up the road.
It's a shame to waste it.
One day I want to live there.
Gordon's going to go for Deputy Chief Constable of
Highlands and Islands region. That's Inverness but I told
him he can fly to work every morning in a microlight.
Gordon's a DIY junkie.
The children can go to school on the Internet.
I'll croft.
I'm learning Gaelic.
This little one's going to go to a Gaelic primary school.
Because it would be a waste not to learn another language.
And it's Scottish too.
So it'd be a waste if nobody speaks it.
A waste of all those place names.
A waste of all that poetry.

What do you do, Viv?

Vivienne   I'm a speech therapist.

Claire   The things you can do.
One can do.
You'll have to tell me about it sometime.

Vivienne   It's not terribly interesting, I'm afraid.

Claire   Oh no, Viv. It is. Everything's interesting if you're interested in people. That's why I joined the police. It's a people job. Like yours probably.

Vivienne   I help people who can't communicate. For medical reasons.

Claire   Viv. Do you mind? It's boiling, isn't it. Sweltering. I'm going to put the kettle on and boil us up a cup of refreshing herbal tea.

Vivienne   I don't know if I –

Claire   Really it's just the chat, isn't it?
Girls together.
Talking about little ones.
I bet you've got some stories.
Would you mind just finishing this off for me, Viv?
I'll only be a tic.

She hands **Vivienne** *the trowel.*

Vivienne   Thank you.

Claire   Just a wee second and then we can have a nice chat over a cuppa.

Claire *leaves.* **Vivienne** kneels *and begins to dig with the trowel as* **Claire** *was doing. She stops. Looks around her. An aeroplane passes overhead.*

Vivienne   Claire?

. . .

She tries to dig again.
She stands up.

Vivienne   Claire?

She drops the trowel.

Claire?

10

In the airport.

Keith *and* **Eric** *at a bar in Heathrow airport.*

Keith   I get drunk. Can I be honest with you? I can't control myself. Something wild rises up in me and I just talk to anybody. I tell the truth. I tell lies. Whatever. I met this Russian girl, the one I was telling you about, in this club that's supposed to be a place where film people go or something. She was dancing a striptease to 'Je t'aime' (*He sings a portion of this tune.*) and when she came over to my table so I could give her some money I told her it was my favourite piece of music, which it isn't. It's just . . . a piece of music I know, but I wanted to have something kind to say to her. I just wanted to say something kind.

. . . She's much younger than me.

I'm under no illusions about her motivation. But something . . .

Have another whisky.

Barman, two Ardbeg.

In Gaelic, 'whisky' means water of life.

I seem to be able to talk to anyone over a whisky.

If only you could sit down with everybody over a whisky. If only every single encounter was just two people, and a wooden table and a whisky.

It's tearing me apart to be honest with you. It really is. I'm shaken up.

You Norwegians suppress, don't you? You're Calvinist? Norwegians?

Fish. Oil. Silence and Fear.

You're just like us Scots.

When I was young I thought I'd be free of it, not like my

father. I travelled the entire fucking world. I lived in foreign
cities. Work camps in the middle of Amazonia. The desert.
Even the middle of the fucking sea. I thought I'd escaped. But
it steals over you, doesn't it, like a damp towel over a flame.
Fucking life.

. . .

I can taste every inch of her body, you know.
I can smell every inch of her body.
The tiny blemish on her thigh.
The scar on her forehead.
Listen to this.

He takes out a hand-held mini tape recorder and presses play.

I recorded the sound of her breathing when she was asleep.

Eric   She sounds perfect.

Keith   I'm under no illusions.

Eric   Play it again.

Keith *plays it again.*

Eric   You're a lucky man.

Keith   I can tell you this, Eric.
I know the value of this.
I know how much it costs.

Eric   I would pay you for that tape.

Keith   You want it?

Eric   How much is it worth?

Keith   Are you joking?

Eric   No.

. . .

Of course I'm joking.

They relax a little.

You're a lucky man.

11

On *board the Harmony 114.*

Casimir I'm sorry.
About before.

Oleg Me too, comrade.
We were carried away by our emotions.
It's inevitable from time to time.

Casimir One day, soon, I'll succeed in killing you.

Oleg Or me you.

Casimir If it happens.
Then I'm sorry.

Oleg I understand.

Casimir If I kill you, Oleg.
And then by some miracle, I'm rescued.
What should I do?
Should I contact anyone?

Oleg First . . . tell the Soviet people I died for them,
proudly.

Casimir All right.
I'll tell them.

Oleg Secondly, there's a woman –

12

In the airport bar.

Keith Where are you flying to, Eric?

Eric The Middle East.

Keith Business, or pleasure?

Eric I'm negotiating a peace treaty between two warring
factions. It's an extremely complex situation. I can't say too

much about it at this stage. The factions don't want to admit
they're talking to each other. It would be interpreted as a sign
of weakness by their supporters. The factions have been at war
for decades. Really, thousands and thousands of lives have
been wasted.

Keith   Nasty.

Eric   It's quite an unpleasant task, Keith.
The men I'm negotiating with . . .
Truthfully, they're vicious animal bastards with absolutely no
compassion.

Keith   I hate that type of person.

Eric   So do I, Keith. So do I. But . . . someone's got to talk
to them.

Keith   Is that what you do?
Is that your job?
Negotiating.

Eric   I work for the World Bank.

Keith   Oh right.

Eric   I'm a civil servant, Keith, just like you.

Keith   Different class from me, Eric, I'm afraid.

Eric   No, the same. Species – servant, genus – civil. We are
the people who maintain order. Isn't that right? We know
that, left to itself nature is attracted towards chaos. We know
that, left to itself human life descends into violence, atrocity,
and injustice. We serve. We civilise. It's not a job people
admire, it's boring, maybe even despicable but people like us,
Keith, are the bulwark against the flood. Isn't that right?

Keith   I work in fisheries.

Eric   Then you'll understand precisely what I'm talking
about.

Keith   These men you have to talk to . . .

Eric   Terrible people, Keith. Killers. Awful.

Keith There has to be a moment when . . . you can't carry
on in the face of that kind of mentality. You have the chance,
you have to meet with these people. You could take a gun into
one of these meetings.

Eric A gun?

Keith You could kill them both.
Even if you died . . .

Eric But . . .

Keith It would be an act of heroism.

Eric I don't want to die.

Keith No but . . . a chance to do something absolutely
good.
Imagine.
How many of us have that chance.

Eric Look. I'm optimistic. At least they're talking.

Keith I would kill them.

Eric I understand your attitude, Keith, but it's a matter of
leaving things behind, isn't it? We bring these men together in
a room with a wooden table. We bring them whisky and we
talk it over until – and you should see them when this
happens, Keith, it's astonishing – they realise that the chaos of
their lives can simply be left behind. They accept. Their eyes,
Keith, are full of relief. It's very moving.

Keith I never thought of it that way.

Eric Do you mind me talking in a personal way with you?

Keith Not at all, Eric.

Eric Keith, I want to tell you . . .
There's no need for things to be difficult for you.
There's no need for you to be unhappy.
No need.

Keith No?

Eric   This is my job.
To see this.

Keith   It's a different situation in my case, Eric.
I'm –

Eric   You can accept, Keith.

Keith   I'm not involved in killing anybody.

Eric   You're killing yourself.

Something of a pause.
Keith *takes out a business card.*

Keith   This is her name.

He writes a name and address.

This is where you can find her.

He gives the card to **Eric.**
Eric *takes it.*
An airport tannoy announcement.

Tannoy   This is the last call for Mr Keith Sutherland
travelling to Edinburgh on flight BA230E. Will Mr Sutherland
please make his way to Gate 15 immediately. This is the last
call for passenger Sutherland travelling to Edinburgh on
BA230E. Will passenger Keith Sutherland please make his
way to Gate 15 immediately.

Keith   You won't tell anyone what I said, will you?

Eric   Of course not, you neither?

Keith   Never. You'll never tell anyone you met me?

Eric   Never. You?

Keith   Never.
Let's celebrate.
Let's have another whisky.
One for the road.

Eric   To life!
You know, in Norway we also have a drink called 'water of

life'. Maybe, every country in the world calls its strongest
drink by that name.

13

On a small stage, **Nastasja** *and* **Sylvia**. **Nastasja** *is dancing
erotically to a version of 'Je t'aime moi non plus' which has been treated
with a dance drum track. She is not really trying.* **Sylvia** *is dressed as
though to dance erotically but she barely moves.*

14

On board the spacecraft.

Oleg   This woman . . . we were at school together.
I was in love with her.
I followed her around like a sick dog.
She and her friends teased me about it but I could not be
diverted.
Then, when I went to the military academy, I thought about
her every day. Until, one weekend on home leave, I met her
again.
No longer a schoolgirl.
We laughed about old times.
She invited me to her flat.
We spent a beautiful weekend together.
It was the most perfect weekend of my life.
We were made for each other.
We touched each other's souls.
I went back to my barracks a changed man.
I intended to contact her the next week but . . .
What can I say?
I was busy. I simply didn't get round to it. Ridiculous.
And then, you know, when I finally sat down to call her . . .
Well, you know how it is . . .
We had touched each other's souls. I couldn't just say . . .
'I'm sorry, I forgot to call . . .' No.

For days I tried to figure out an excuse.
By now I realised she would be angry and hurt.
I didn't know what to do.
After a month had passed I realised I'd have to have a very
good reason for my silence.
And then . . .
Years and years and years seemed to just . . . go.
And now.
If I die, and, by some miracle you're rescued.
I'd like you to find this woman and say . . .
'Oleg's last words to me were . . .
"Tell Adrianna" he said . . . "Tell Adrianna . . . "'
Wait a minute . . .
Tell her my last words were . . .
Maybe I should try to write them down.

Casimir   You know, Oleg.
She has most probably forgotten you.

Oleg   I haven't forgotten her.

Casimir Most probably she doesn't care in the slightest.

Oleg   I feel bad about what I did.

Casimir   Most probably she's long ago ceased feeling any
pain on the subject.

Oleg   The words will be in an envelope in my locker.

Casimir   She's down there somewhere.
Living her life.
Where are we?

Oleg *moves to the window.*

Oleg   We're over Europe, moving into the night.

15

A street in London.

Dusk. **Nastasja** *dressed in an elegant and expensive evening outfit.*
The sound of an aeroplane overhead.

Nastasja *shouts at the aeroplane.*

Nastasja   LIAR! LIAR! YOU LIAR!
What are you looking at, you English pigs.
Haven't you ever heard a woman shout before?
No. Of course you haven't.
You put pillows in their mouths.
LIAR! LIAR! YOU FUCK SHIT LIAR!

16

In a café in Provence.

Bernard *is standing at the counter, reading a newspaper, with the*
Proprietor.

Bernard   Have you seen this?
The Americans want to write the word 'Pepsi' in space.
A giant advertisement.
To say 'Pepsi'.
Every night it will compete with the moon.

Proprietor   The moon has nothing to sell.

Bernard   Give me a whisky.

Proprietor   It makes good business sense.
Scotch or Bourbon?

Bernard   Don't give me any of that filthy Bourbon.
I'll smash it over your counter.
Give me a Scottish malt.
(*He toasts.*)
Death to the Americans!

Proprietor   I like Americans.

244   The cosmonaut's last message . . .

Bernard   Americans are poison. They colonise our minds.

Proprietor   On the contrary, Bernard, they're energetic
and friendly, and their money is good.
I welcome Americans.

Bernard   I shun them.

Proprietor   What about Elvis?
Do you shun Elvis?

Bernard   Without reservation.

Proprietor   What about Hank Williams!

Bernard   What about Dostoevsky!

Proprietor   What about Walt Whitman!

Bernard   What about Jean Genet!

Proprietor   What about John Wayne!

Bernard   What about Gainsbourg!

Proprietor   What about *West Side Story?*

Bernard   What about Oedipus!

Proprietor   What about . . .

Bernard   What about . . .
What about . . .

Proprietor   What about . . .

Bernard   If you want my custom you'd better shut your
mouth.

Proprietor   . . .
. . .

Martin Scorcese . .

Bernard   Don Quixote.

Proprietor   OK.

Bernard   OK.

Proprietor   OK.
Just remember, Bernard. If you choose to cease drinking in
my bar. Know this.
I will not mourn.
For every Frenchman, there are a thousand Americans who
are friendly and whose money is always good.

Bernard   One day, I tell you this, there will come a time
when all the stories humanity has ever told will have been
made into films set in American high schools.

Proprietor   I look forward to that day.

Bernard   I can no longer speak to you.
You're an Uncle Tom.

Proprietor   In the scheme of things it's not important.

Bernard   Fuck you.

Proprietor   I'm sorry.

Bernard   So you say.

Proprietor   You have to learn to accept, Bernard.
You'll have another stroke.
. . .
OK.
I'm sorry.
You know I only like to disagree.
If there's a proposition – I disagree with it.
It's a way of living.
. . .
Of course, in reality, Americans repulse me.

Bernard   OK.

Proprietor   You're a valued customer.

Bernard   Thank you.

Proprietor   You're welcome.

They shake hands.

Now. Bernard.

Tell me about the sky.
Have you made contact yet?

Bernard   I've moved my equipment further up the mountain.
The light pollution is less.
It's been too cloudy recently.
The craft is there but I've been unable to open communication.

Proprietor   Perhaps these visitors . . . perhaps they don't understand French.

Bernard   I've been transmitting equations.
Simple geometry, prime numbers, pi.

Proprietor   Lucky I'm not an alien then.
Geometry is a foreign language to me.

Bernard   They're here to teach us something.
I'm sure of it.
A secret. A secret.
They have a higher intelligence.
If only I can find the right language.

Proprietor   Have you tried broadcasting erotica?

Bernard   No.

Proprietor   It might work.
A picture of a woman.
It's a universally understood symbol.

Bernard   They have wisdom.

Proprietor   How do you know?

Bernard   Their silence tells me.
Their silence in the face of . . . what they must see.
They're waiting till we stop.
And look up.
And realise.
And find the right words.

Proprietor   Listen, Bernard. You read the papers.

Maybe these aren't aliens at all.
You know. Between you and me.
They throw all kinds of shit at the sky.

Bernard   I'm certain.
I've checked all the data.
I contacted a friend of mine at the Space Agency.
I asked him to identify it.
I said, 'Look, you know me. I'm no terrorist. If this is just some spy satellite. Tell me. Put my mind at rest. Let me sleep in my bed at night.'
But no.
He had no explanation.

Proprietor   They say . . . don't they . . . you worked in this field . . . is it true these spy satellites can take pictures in which you can see the face of the playing card a man's holding? The tiniest blemish on a woman's skin? Is it true they can see?

Bernard   It's true.

Proprietor   I don't know, Bernard. If I didn't like you. If you weren't such a valued customer I'd ban you. Coming in here with these stories. They put the wind right up me. I was making love to Louise in the open air only last week. What if they took one of these photographs? What if it reached my wife?

Bernard   It's perfectly possible that this craft contains all the secrets of mankind.

Proprietor   And they say nothing?

Bernard   What can they say?

Proprietor   What sort of mentality is . . . what sort of cunt is it that wants to know these things about me? What sort of cunt wants to hold these secrets like an axe over my head. I'm an honest man.
. . .
I don't believe in it.

Bernard   Come with me.

They go out into the square.

The craft is above us now.
Look. See.
Can you see it moving?

Proprietor   I think so.

Bernard   Just below Orion's belt, moving eastwards.

Proprietor   The bastard. There it is.
. . .
They know about me.

Bernard   Everything.

Proprietor   And they say nothing?

Bernard   Not a word.

Proprietor   How can they possibly . . .

Bernard   They can. It's possible.

17

A garden in the grounds of a hospital.

Vivienne *is visiting the* **Patient**.

Vivienne   Can you tell me what day it is today, Joe?

Patient   No. No. I can't tell you that no. I'm sorry.

Vivienne   Can you tell me what year it is?

Patient   Ehm . . . No. No. I'm ever so sorry. No.

Vivienne   Can you tell me what happened yesterday, Joe?
Can you tell me what you had for breakfast?

Patient   Awww fuck. I knew you'd . . . I knew you'd . . .
ohhhh ya bugger. No, love. I'm awful sorry. I'm sorry. It's no
there, love.

Vivienne   Where are you just now, Joe? Can you tell me
that?

Patient   I think I'm . . . the stuff's a clue, isn't it?
And . . . the the the wood TREES are a clue . . . fuck.

Vivienne   You're in the garden, Joe. In the garden.

Patient   That's right. That'll be it.

Vivienne   What can you tell me about the garden?

Patient   . . .
. . .
. . .
She comes running towards me on that stuff.
That beautiful stuff.
She comes running towards me.
Ma feet on that lovely stuff.
Awww it feels nice.
And she's smiling so she is.
Aye.
Awww that lovely stuff.
She comes running over here.
And she's smiling so she is.
. . .

Vivienne   Grass, Joe?

Patient   Fuck aye. That's it.
She comes running towards me, aye . . . on that lovely grass.

Vivienne   Is this a long time ago, Joe?

Patient   Of course it is. Fuck aye.
She's running. Fuck aye.

Vivienne   Who, Joe? Who comes running?

Patient   Oh God.
. . .
No. Sorry. Fuck. No. I'm awful sorry, love. No.

18

A bar in Soho, London.

It's a quiet night. **Sylvia** *and* **Nastasja** *alone together.*

Sylvia   Have a Pepsi.

. . .

This is how men are, Nastasja.
They lie without even thinking about it. They don't even think
they're lying when they lie. This is the thing. They think
they're telling the truth. They see the world differently,
Nastasja.
Shh.
I love you. C'mon.
You know I'll never leave you.
When men see life, Nastasja, they see it through their own
eyes. They're missing from the picture, do you understand,
like the camera in a film.
When we see life, we're in the film, talking, being looked at . . .
we understand about life, Nastasja, because we're in it.

. . .

Cry on my shoulder.
That's it.

. . .

Men think the entire world is contained in their eyes,
Nastasja, they think you disappear when their eyes leave
you.
Why don't you take the night off.
Why don't you stay with me.
Let me look after you.

. . .

Always.
I promise.

Nastasja   Why do they have to go?
Why can't they come back?
They say.
They only say.

19

On board the Harmony 114.

Oleg *is holding a playing card.*
The music of a Soviet choir is playing.
Casimir *is attempting to fix the radio.*

Casimir Bring me the second suit.

Oleg Why?

Casimir The first suit is damaged.

Oleg They're both damaged.

Casimir The second suit is less damaged.

Oleg Why do you want a suit at all?

Casimir I'm going out.

Oleg Out? Where?

Casimir Out.

Oleg It's too dangerous.

Casimir I'm going to try to fix the communications.

Oleg You know yourself it's too dangerous.

Casimir I want to talk to my daughter.

Oleg It's suicide.

Casimir I want to talk to someone.

Oleg Talk to me.
Talk to me about . . .

Casimir I don't want to talk to you about anything any
more.
I want to be rescued.

Oleg No one will rescue us.
We've been forgotten.

Casimir If I send a message, someone will hear it.

Oleg   No one is listening.

Casimir   How can they listen if we're not communicating?

Oleg   What if it's the Americans?

Casimir   I love America
I want to drink Pepsi Cola.
I want to see sex shows.
I want to go to New York and open a restaurant.

Oleg   The Americans may decide to kill us.

Casimir   I yearn to be killed by an American.

Oleg   They might use us as pawns against our own people.

Casimir   I want to talk to somebody.

Oleg   WE HAVE NO AUTHORISATION TO COMMUNICATE.
The mission is secret.

Casimir   We completed the mission.
Nobody has contacted us for twelve years.

Oleg   The mission is still secret.
The order has not been countermanded.

Casimir   I want to talk to my daughter.
Give me the suit.

Oleg   We have a responsibility.
Let's talk about this picture.
Let's talk about her.

Casimir   No more.

Oleg   If you make contact, what will you say?

Casimir   Please let me talk to my children.

Oleg   Your daughter has forgotten you.

Casimir   When she hears my voice she'll remember.

Oleg   Nobody welcomes a ghost into their house, Casimir.

Casimir   I'm alive.

Oleg   You'll destroy her.

Casimir   I love her.

Oleg   She's made life without you.
Return is not possible.
You can't go back.
We can't go back and we can't go forward.
We can only . . .
Carry on.
The time lines have diverged.
. . .
Take the card.
Let's talk.

Casimir   Give me the second suit.

20

A beach, near Edinburgh.

A car pulls up, its headlights on full beam. The headlights illuminate two broad strips of beach and sea cutting deeply into the night sky. It's raining. The car radio is playing 'To Live is to Fly' by Townes Van Zandt.

Keith *gets out of the car and walks, in the headlight beam towards the sea.*
He takes off his clothes and folds them.
He is naked.
He takes out the tape recorder and plays the tape of **Nastasja** *breathing. Above him, in the stars, the satellite continues its orbit.*

21

The house in Edinburgh.

Vivienne *shuts the large shutters. She sits on the sofa. She switches the television on.*

Static.

22

On board the Harmony module.

Oleg *looking at the card.*
Oleg *listens.*
Casimir*'s excited voice comes through some kind of intercom.*

Casimir   I'm getting something.
I can hear . . .
Oleg, I can hear something . . .
I can hear a voice, Oleg.
Speech . . . in some language I . . .
I can hear a voice.
Hello? Hello?
Numbers, Oleg.
Hundreds of numbers.
Numbers in different languages.
Harmony.
114.
Harmony.
114.
Harmony.
114.

The sound of a Soviet choir.

Act Two

1

A garden on a mountainside in Provence.
Darkness.
The sound of wind blowing through the trees.
The stars appear.
One star is moving, describing a slow arc across the sky.
The sound of radio static.
Through the static we can just make out **Casimir***'s voice.*

Casimir   ... *Harmony 114 ... Harmony 114 ...*
(*Breathing.*)
Harmony ...

A computer.
Bernard *enters.*

Darkness becomes early dawn. It has been a long night. **Bernard** *is the worse for it. His computer, attached to a small satellite dish, is set up on a small porch in his garden. The detritus of the night is piled up around him.* **Bernard** *is playing with a computer programme that has recorded the sound picked up from the satellite. He plays and then replays the recording of* **Casimir***.*

He types.
After he has typed, an automated voice plays what he has typed.

Voice   *Harmony?*
Please.
What is harmony?
Is harmony music?
Do you want music?
I don't understand.
Please help me.
I want to talk to you.
I want to make contact.
Please help me.
Static.

Bernard   Why won't you talk to me, you motherfuckers?

2

A room in a police station in Edinburgh.

Claire *and* **Vivienne** *are sitting on opposite sides of a table.*
Claire *is in her policewoman's uniform.*
Between them is a neatly folded pile of **Keith***'s clothes.*
The tie is folded on the top.

Claire   This must be just awful for you, Viv.
. . .
Take your time.
. . .
Because we have to be sure.
. . .
Don't we?

Vivienne   Yes.

Claire   These are the clothes we found.

Vivienne   Yes.

Claire   Are they your husband's clothes, Viv?

Vivienne   Yes.

Claire   Is this his tie?

She takes the tie. Hands it to **Vivienne**. **Vivienne** *holds it.
Studies it.*

Vivienne   I think so.

Claire   Are you sure?
It's quite an unusual tie, isn't it?

Vivienne   He bought it. I normally buy his ties.
He bought a tie just like this one.
He was wearing it.

Claire   You normally buy his ties?

Vivienne   Normally.

Claire   But you didn't buy this one?

Vivienne   No.
I don't like it.
I'm not a connoisseur.
But I don't like the picture.

Claire   No.

Vivienne   It's brash.

Claire   I know.

Vivienne   Keith isn't a brash man.
The tie didn't suit him.
That's why I noticed it.
I wouldn't buy a tie like that.
I prefer his clothes to be . . .

Claire   Understated.

Vivienne   Yes.

Claire   And you noticed this tie because it was brash?

Vivienne   Keith's dead.

Claire   Do you think you could identify this as *his* tie, Viv?

Vivienne   It's definitely his.

Claire   I'm sorry, Viv.
This must be awful for you.

Vivienne   It couldn't be he lent it to someone?
. . .
No.

Claire   We can't rule anything out. Not at this stage.

Vivienne   He doesn't swim.
And the water.
 . . . so cold.
He . . .

Claire   Have you had any . . . indication, Viv?
Any sense that he was troubled.

Vivienne   He always seems troubled.
Things trouble him.

Claire   Did he seem especially troubled?
Did he seem unhappy, Viv?

Vivienne   Only in as much as . . .
I mean.
A certain amount of unhappiness is . . .
Normal.
For us.

Claire   Sometimes if a man is in trouble. He feels
pressure . . .
He feels . . .
Forces acting on him . . .
He . . .

Vivienne   Keith's strong. He's a rock. I've always said that.
A rock.

Claire   You said he was troubled.

Vivienne   He's a rock.
He's troubled.
He's both things.

Claire   Forces act on rocks, Viv.
A man's mind.
Can create forces that . . .

Vivienne   How do you know?

Claire   We receive training.

Vivienne   Don't you think I know my husband?

Claire   Nobody *knows* him, Viv.
That's the awful thing.
Nobody knows the particular forces . . .
Was he in debt?

Vivienne No.

Claire Sex. A sexual thing?

Vivienne It's not possible.

Claire A vague worry?

Vivienne No.

Claire A nagging worry?

Vivienne Everything is normal. Everything is – was –
normal. Obviously it wasn't normal. I'm not a fool, Claire.
Clearly if my husband has walked into the sea that isn't
normal. But . . .
It was normal.
Do you understand?
Is this normal?
This walking into the sea?
Do other people do it?

Claire It's been known. A man drives his car to the beach.
He takes his clothes off and leaves them neatly piled up. He
leaves the car headlights on so the vehicle is easily found and
then . . .

Vivienne He walks into the sea.

Claire He disappears.

Vivienne He was alone. He must have been scared.

Claire This must be awful for you.
Vivienne –
But, you know, he may not be dead.

Vivienne He can't swim. He can't bloody swim. I know my
husband.

Claire He withdrew a large amount of money, Viv.
From your bank account. Over two thousand pounds. No
money was found in these clothes.

Vivienne Do you think he's . . .
What do you mean 'may not be dead'?

Claire   Everything is . . . a form of signal, Viv.
The clothes.
The money.

Vivienne   The clothes?

Claire   The suit. The way it's folded so neatly. That's him telling us that this was a considered action. That he's thought about it. Do you see? The money, he must have wanted to take the money with him.

Vivienne   You're saying he's lost. The poor man he's . . .

Claire The clothes were in a place they would be found.

Vivienne   We should look for him. We must . . . you. You're the police. You're . . .

Claire   He doesn't want to be found. That's what he's telling us.

Vivienne   But he's alive?

Claire   We don't *know*. We can't *know*.

Vivienne   He's trying to talk to me.

Claire   He's talking to all of us.

Vivienne   The suit is a message?

Claire   Yes.

Vivienne   Saying that he's alive?

Claire   The message doesn't say that.

Vivienne   He's going to come back?

Claire   The suit says . . . 'I want to seem dead.'

Vivienne   Only seem dead. Only seem.

Claire   You have to remember, Viv, that one way of seeming dead is to be dead.

Vivienne But . . .

Claire The tie, Viv.
Tell me about the tie.

Vivienne Tell you?

Claire The tie is a signal directed at you, Viv.
He's telling you something.
He knew it was a signal you would understand.

Vivienne But I didn't. *You* told me.

Claire I've been trained.
The picture on the tie. There's a label. It says . . .
'Mont Saint Victoire' by Paul Cézanne.
Does that mean anything to you?

Vivienne No.

Claire Do you know this name . . . Paul Cézanne?

Vivienne Of course I do. He's the artist. The artist
Cézanne.

Claire I know that, Viv. I knew you would know.
But we have to be sure.
It's . . .
. . .
OK.
OK.
Maybe it's a coincidence.
Maybe the picture . . .
Maybe it's some kind of message we don't understand.

Vivienne *begins to cry without drama.*
Claire *reaches out a hand to hold hers.*
They hold hands.

Something of a pause.

Vivienne *gathers herself.*
She takes her hand back.
Claire *withdraws her own hand a moment later.*

Vivienne   He was a rock.

Claire   What he's done to you, Viv.
It's a crime.

Vivienne   But he was troubled.

Claire   To abandon your life. It's wrong. We can't do that.
You'll find yourself becoming angry.

Vivienne   I'm not angry.

Claire   We get this. It's a people job, Viv.
It's part of our training to stand back.
To protect ourselves as much as anything.
But I look at you and the agony you're in.
It makes me angry.

Vivienne   I'm just taken aback, Claire. I'm just . . .

Claire   It's such a waste . . . such a waste because . . .
Someone else could have had his life, Viv.

Vivienne   Do you think I was a cause?

Claire   Who knows?

Vivienne   I could have been a vague force. A vague worry.
A nagging worry. Maybe I was acting on him. All these years
until –

Claire   No doubt you were part of it, Viv. But it's beyond
me.
We're friends. So luckily I can be honest with you.
But if only he'd said something.

Vivienne   But he didn't. He didn't say anything.

Claire   It could have been sorted out.
Just talking. Just to talk.
Murder, Vivienne. Suicide. All types of crime could be wiped
out if people only talked.
I have a terrible bee in my bonnet about this.
But it really is such an awful awful waste.

Vivienne   The television had broken.

Claire   I'm sorry?

Vivienne   It was the only thing that wasn't normal.
The television broke and we . . . talked about . . . nothing in
particular and we opened the shutters and . . .
That was the only thing that wasn't normal, Claire.
. . .
I'm going to get rid of the television.
I'm going to read more.
Or music.
It's so long since I've actually *read* anything.

3

On board the Harmony 114 module.

Oleg *is dictating the ship's log.*

Oleg   The communication system is now destroyed with no
possibility of repair.
Comrade Casimir's attempt to repair the communication
system failed.
I am unable either to receive or transmit.
Comrade Casimir is no longer . . . with me.
Life-support systems are working.
I have rations.
I now have Comrade Casimir's rations as well as mine.
My survival is assured indefinitely.
Until the mission ends.
. . .
This is the end of today's log entry.

Oleg *switches off the machine.*

*From his pocket he draws a pack of cards with pictures of women on
them.*
He holds a hand of cards.
He chooses a card.

4

A dingy underground bar in Soho, London.

A version of Albinoni's 'Adagio' mixed with an electronic backbeat plays loudly.
Sylvia *is standing on the stage.* **Sylvia** *is dressed as though to dance erotically but she doesn't dance. She barely moves.*
Eric *is watching.*
Nastasja *is sitting at* **Eric**'s *table. She's wearing a black cocktail dress and high heels. She's heavily made up.*
He puts his arm around her waist.

Something of a pause.

She shouts. The music is loud.

Nastasja   I wish they'd switch off this fucking shit, mister!

Eric   What!

Nastasja   I said I . . .

She walks up to **Sylvia** *and says something to her privately.* **Sylvia** *leaves the stage. A moment or two later the music stops.* **Nastasja** *returns to* **Eric.**

It's a fucking tomb in here. Where is everybody.
Do you see any film stars, mister.
Sometimes they come down and look at us.
Are you some kind of film star.

Eric   No.
Are you?

Nastasja   No.

Eric   I'm surprised.

Nastasja   What are you, mister? If you're not a film star?
I know you, don't I?
You direct films? You a cameraman?

Eric   I have nothing to do with films. I don't even watch them.

Nastasja   You want champagne?

Eric   No.

Nastasja   I want champagne.
Sylvia!
Bring some drinks.
Maybe you write films then?
Your face looks like a face I know.

Eric   I don't think we've ever met. Sadly.

Nastasja   You're police, mister.
You know I'm not some fuck shit English girl.

Eric   It's to your credit.

Nastasja   I'm Russian.

Sylvia *brings a glass of champagne.*

Nastasja   What you drinking, mister?

Eric   Vodka, please.

Nastasja   You're so polite, mister.
You come down here to be polite?
You work in the theatre?

Eric   I'm afraid not.

Nastasja One day. I'll tell you the story of my life. I'll write it
for a play and they'll make it into a worldwide film. My
daddy's up in the sky. He went there when I was six years old.
I learned the part of Hedda Gabler written by Henrik Ibsen.
They didn't let me in to the theatre school because I was too
young. I always thought my daddy would come back. He
never has.
What's the weather like up there?
Is it daylight?
Or can you see the stars?

Eric   It's sunny and clear with a slight breath of wind.

Nastasja   I haven't been up in the city for days. You forget.
One forgets.

Eric   What's your name?

Nastasja   Nastasja. I'm from Russia. I'm not some fuck shit English girl with a pillow over my mouth. Listen, mister, the price they charge you for champagne down here. Can you imagine it. Sixty pounds.

Eric   Is that expensive?

Nastasja   You don't mind?

Eric *takes out his wallet. He holds a small bundle of notes.*

Eric   I don't even know what one of these is worth. I seem to have hundreds of them in my wallet.

Nastasja   Are you rich, mister?

Eric   I'm Norwegian.

Nastasja   What are you doing in this place? Are you some kind of Norwegian film producer?

Eric   The world of cinema is completely foreign to me.

Nastasja   What are you doing in London then?

Eric   I love London.

Nastasja So do I!

Eric   I love meeting new people.

Nastasja   Me too!

Eric   My job takes me to most of the major cities of the world.
Some of the minor ones even.
But of all the cities I've visited I love London the most.
You know, I buy my tea in London.
I go to Fortnum and Mason's.
Sometimes I buy rare and second-hand books on the Charing Cross Road or electronic goods from Tottenham Court Road.
If I want to buy toys for my nieces and nephews: Hamleys.
Spending money is always a pleasure in London.
That's my opinion.

Nastasja   It's my opinion too.

Eric   This currency means nothing to me.
It feels lighter than dollars.
Like it could fly away on the slightest breath of wind.

Sylvia comes with more drinks.

Nastasja   It's dead down here, mister.
It's a fucking tomb.

Eric   Would you like to go somewhere else?

Nastasja   Anywhere, mister.
Anywhere you want as long as it's up there.
Will you take me?

Eric   Of course.
If you excuse me one moment.
I have to make a call.

He takes out a mobile phone.

Sylvia   That thing won't work down here.
You'll get no signal.

Eric   I see.

Sylvia   You can use the phone at the bar.

Eric   Thank you.
I'll only be a moment.

Eric *exits.*

Nastasja   Why did you do that, you fucking shitty English?

Sylvia   What?

Nastasja   Send him away.

Sylvia   I didn't.
He wanted to make a call.

Nastasja   You sent him away.

Eric *has left his wallet on the table.* **Sylvia** *looks at the wallet. She looks at the amount of money.*

Nastasja   Don't steal his money.

Sylvia   Why not?

Nastasja   He'll come back.
He'll take me up there with him.

Sylvia   You can't go. You're working.

Nastasja   I asked him to take me.
He said he would.

Sylvia *looks pained.*

Nastasja *holds her.*

Nastasja   Don't worry.

Eric *returns from the phone.*

Nastasja   Mister, I can't go anywhere just now. I'm working.

Eric   Not anymore.

Nastasja   No. You don't understand, mister.

Eric   I've made certain calls to certain people.

Nastasja   Which people? Did you talk to my boss?

Eric   I talked to certain people who employ the people who employ your boss. I've made certain arrangements.
Everything is all right now.

Nastasja   Where are you taking me?

Eric   Wherever you want. London belongs to you.

5

The garden of a hospital.

The **Patient** *is sitting on a bench.* **Vivienne** *approaches him.*

Vivienne   How are you today, Joe?

Patient   . . . Sad . . .

Vivienne   I'm sorry to hear that.

Patient   Sad.

Vivienne   Why are you sad, Joe? Has anything happened? Is there a reason?

Patient (*an effort to understand / explain*)   I'm sorry . . . no.
No.
. . .
Sad love. Sad.
No.

Vivienne   You don't have to explain, Joe, if you can't . . .

Patient (*a huge effort to explain. He gestures at the garden. The world*)
Oh yes . . . that stuff . . . and that stuff . . . and oh yes . . .
. . .
Look at that fucking lovely stuff.
Oh yes. Sad.
. . .
FUCK!
Sorry, love.
. . .
Can't. No. No. I'm sorry. I've lost it. FUCK!

Vivienne   It's all right. You're doing very well.

Patient   Buggerit.

The **Patient** *gets up and walks away.*

Vivienne   It's all right.
I understand.

6

A bench in the park in Soho Square.

Nastasja *and* **Eric**. **Nastasja** *is surrounded by bags of expensive shopping and packages.*

Nastasja   I feel alive. The breeze on my face.
I spend too much time in that shitty tomb.
I need to feel alive.

Eric   You don't need to go back.

Nastasja   I know.

Eric   I can buy you anything you want.

Nastasja   I don't want anything.

Eric   All these things?

Nastasja   I wanted them when I saw them.

Eric   You don't want them now?

Nastasja   No. Looking at them now I feel nothing for them.
Are you insulted?

Eric   No. I understand. I feel the same way about them.

Nastasja   I wanted them so much, I felt fucking shitty.
Now I don't feel shitty. I feel free of them.
I feel alive.

Eric   People say we should rid ourselves of our desires. Some
people say that's the way to be happy.

Nastasja   I believe those people.

Eric   But I have found that the only way to get rid of desire.
Is to possess the thing you want.
When you have it, you no longer want it.
Then you're truly free.

Nastasja   You need a lot of money to follow that
philosophy.

Eric   Oh yes.
That's why it only works for a very few people in the world.

Nastasja   What do you want?

Eric   I want you.

Nastasja   Here I am.

Eric   I want you in a deeper way.

Nastasja   Every man I've met said the same thing.

Eric   I want you to come to Oslo with me.
I want to buy you a flat in the centre of the city.

. . .

. . .

What's she doing here?

Sylvia *has entered. She stands at a distance from the other two.*
Watching them.

Nastasja   She's been following us.

Eric   I don't like her here. I didn't like her in the club,
either.

Nastasja   She's my friend.

Eric   I'm sorry.
Should I call her over?

Nastasja   No. Let her stand there.

Eric   She's older than you.

Nastasja   She looks after me.

Eric   She looks like a crow. I don't like her.

Nastasja   She's had a hard life.

Eric   So what?

Nastasja   She has scars on her body.
Sometimes men ask specifically if they can see her dance.
They like to look at the scars.

Eric   The way she's looking at me.
She's like a crow. Or a spider. She's like a spider.

Nastasja   Some time ago, her husband walked into the sea
near the white cliffs of Dover.
Can you imagine?
She was upset.
For a while she wasn't able to cope with life alone.

So she went to France to see if she could find out why he
wanted to swim there.
But all she found was a series of terrible men who resembled
her former husband.
They left her with scars.

Eric   I hate her. Look at her. What is she looking at.
She's criticising me. Your friend is criticising me. The
bitch.

Nastasja   She can't help it. It's just her face.

Eric *gets up. He goes over to* **Sylvia**.

Eric   Look at this crow standing on a branch.
What are you looking at, crow?
How dare you criticise me in front of my girlfriend?
You know nothing about me.
Are you her fucking mother?
You spider.
How much do you cost, spider?
Maybe I want to fuck you.
You're soliciting in a public park I could have you arrested.
Do you do S and M?
That's what I'm into.
So leave it. OK.
Just leave us alone.
Leave us alone you bitch.
She doesn't need you.
She doesn't need you. OK.
Comprendez.
(*Suddenly kind.*)
Look, we don't want this stuff. We have no real need for it.
Why don't you have it. Go on. It's a gift.
It's all yours.
Whore crow.
Right.
OK.
We don't want it any more. So you have it.
You just stand there.
OK.

Shaken, he walks back to **Nastasja** *and sits on the bench beside her.*

I had to say something.
She was begging in a public park.

Nastasja It's just her face.

Eric She was soliciting.
Just because she has nothing she thinks she can threaten the
rest of us.
Jesus.

Nastasja Do you have children, Eric?

Eric No. Do you?

Nastasja No. I want children. Very much.
A little baby boy.

Eric Then you can have one.

Nastasja If I left now, would you follow me?

Eric Yes.

Nastasja How far?

Eric As far as was necessary . . . perhaps myself,
Or maybe I would hire people to do it.
I would ensure that your every movement was supervised.
Videotape made.
Anyone who tried to harm you.
I'd arrange for them to be killed.
That's basically what I'd do.

Nastasja OK, Eric.
I'll come to Oslo with you.

Eric I'll buy you a beautiful flat in the centre of the city.

Nastasja I want to take Sylvia with me.
She looks after me.
She's had a hard life.

Eric OK. She can come too. She can live in the flat with
you. She can be your housekeeper.

Nastasja   OK.
That's OK.

She gets up and leaves.
Eric *follows her.*
They both ignore the packages and shopping bags.
Sylvia *approaches the bench.*
She sits down amongst the shopping.
She takes out some of the clothes and examines them.
She puts an expensive jacket on.

7

On board the Harmony 114.

Oleg *is dictating the log.*

Oleg   . . . This is my third day alone.
Poor Casimir.
He was lonely. He only wanted to talk to his daughter.
Don't you think I want to talk to my daughter?
That's not heroic.
It's pathetic.
Silence is heroic.
To realise the situation and accept is heroic.
You think I'm responsible for his death.
He's responsible. He's responsible for my death.
He has murdered me.
Just like he said he would.
I don't believe in God.
Luckily.
Don't you think I also have people I love?
People I want to talk to.
Who is his daughter that she's so important.
She is most probably some slag whoring herself round the
cities of Europe.
She's most probably a good studious kind girl.
She has most probably forgotten him.
As if anyone else could have talked to him.

Who?

Who can talk to me now?

What language would we use to communicate?

We were dead together.

Now I'm dead alone.

He's in orbit beside me.

I watch the sun reflect off his visor.

Some day.

People, or perhaps visitors from superior planets, will find this log.

They'll find Casimir.

They'll have superior technologies which will perhaps be able to read the remains of brains and decipher them.

To these people of the future . . .

I wish to register.

A salute to my former comrade.

And a message to Adrianna . . .

Adrianna . . .

. . .

I don't remember her second name . . .

Shit.

He switches off the log.

Adrianna . . . ?

Adrianna . . . ?

8

A café in Provence.

Vivienne *is sitting at a café table. The* **Proprietor** *is standing over her.* **Keith**'s *tie is lying on the table. The* **Proprietor** *picks it up.*

Proprietor   That's it. That's the one.

Vivienne   You know it?

Proprietor   I know it well. It's about fifteen kilometres from here.

Vivienne   I wasn't sure if it was real.

Proprietor   How could it not be real?
Could any imagination have invented this?
Don't tell me you could have thought that?
Cézanne made many many attempts to paint this mountain.
This mountain was . . . life.
And he . . . engaged with it.
He struggled.
This mountain was his Everest. His Kachenjunga. His Mont
Blanc.
And you think . . . It's possible to think . . . he invented it?

Vivienne   I'm not a connoisseur.
I don't even like the picture.
I just want to see it for myself.

Proprietor   What do you expect to find?
Are you American?

Vivienne   I'm Scottish. I'm sorry. I didn't mean to . . .

Proprietor   You want to find something? You want to
prove him wrong?

Vivienne   No.

Proprietor   It's fifteen kilometres from here.
See it for yourself if you want.
You will be disappointed.
Everyone is.

Vivienne   Is it possible to . . . is there a hotel? I . . .

Proprietor   You can stay here if you have to.
I will give you a room at a discount.
I like the Scots. They're friendly people and their money is
good.

Vivienne   I . . . thank you . . . that's so kind but . . .
I need to stay . . . for some time . . . near this place . . . as
near as possible.
I need to be . . . in this picture . . .

Proprietor   Ah . . . in . . . in . . . I understand.
Of course.
I apologise.
You're looking for something.
You're searching.

Vivienne   I honestly don't know. I . . . I'm a little lost, in
fact.

Proprietor   Don't try to explain. I understand.

Vivienne   Do you know a place where I can stay?

Proprietor   It's not a hotel.

Vivienne   I don't mind.

Proprietor   I'll make the arrangements for you.
It'll be a pleasure.

9

On board Harmony 114.

Oleg *recording the log.*

Oleg   Adrianna . . . I . . .
(*Rewinds tape.*)
Adrianna, I . . . have found that since I last saw you . . .
You have been on my mind.
In my mind.
(*Rewinds tape.*)
Inhabited my thoughts.
(*Rewinds tape.*)
Sometimes and . . .
. . .
(*Rewinds tape.*)
Adrianna, I would like to say I'm sorry.
. . .
Adrianna . . . I wish I could . . .
The blemish on your thigh. The scar on your forehead from

. . .
(*Rewinds tape.*)
Transmit the feeling . . . I . . .
(*Rewinds tape.*)
I don't love you. Don't think that. I realise I will never see
you again. I don't even want to talk to you face to face . . . if
you don't.
But Adrianna . . .
I just want to say to you . . .
(*Rewinds tape.*)
Adrianna . . .
(*Rewinds tape.*)

10

A room in a flat in central Oslo.

Eric *is looking around. Investigating.*
Sylvia *is sitting in a beautifully made chair.*
The room contains a bed, also beautiful.
The room is perfect. It has doors open on to a balcony.
It is a summer afternoon.
The quieter sound of a small city drifts up.

Eric   Did you do this?

Sylvia   Mostly.

Eric   You did it right. She deserves this. You did it all, didn't
you?

Sylvia   Mostly.

Eric   She deserves it. She won't appreciate it.

Sylvia   I think she likes it.

Eric   Did she say that?

Sylvia   She did.

Eric   She didn't mean it. She said it to please you.

Sylvia   We haven't seen you for a while.

Eric   I've been busy. Working on a treaty.
Landmines.
They're fuckers. They blow the legs off fucking children.
Can you imagine?
I work over there . . . see the window just two above the café?
That's my office.
I look over here sometimes, you know, rest the pencil on the
desk. Switch the phone to mute.
Let the fax machine buzz.
Open the window and I look over here and I think to
myself . . .
. . .
She's . . .
. . .
. . .
I'm going to stop that fucking landmine racket for a start.

Sylvia   I think she missed you.

Eric   I needed to see my wife.

Sylvia   You're not . . . losing interest . . . then?

Eric   What?
You hooded crow.
You woman.
You think I could possibly 'lose interest'?
You think I'm . . .
I'm nowhere close . . .
There are acres of sea between . . .
The horizon comes first between me and . . .
The possibility of not . . .
Not pissing blood at the very thought of her.
You spider.
How dare you call what I feel . . .
How dare you name it.
How dare you even approach the concept of it.
Are you?

Sylvia　What?

Eric　Interested. Still.

Something of a pause.

What does she say to you when you're alone together?

Sylvia　Nothing much. She's only young. She's a bit thick.

Eric　Tell me a thing she says.

Sylvia　Honestly. Nothing worth talking about.

Eric　I can get rid of you at a moment's notice.

. . .

She would be upset.

Sylvia　She makes observations.

Eric *lies on the bed.*

Eric　Tell me.

Sylvia　She says . . . aren't people funny.

. . .

She says she's got no time for churches but she believes God is a personal spirit that blows around us like the wind.

. . .

She says baby girls are more affectionate than baby boys.

. . .

She says isn't it nice to light a candle in a Catholic church.

. . .

She says isn't this song brilliant, isn't it just amazing . . .

Eric　Which song?

Sylvia　I don't know. I don't know about music . . .
She likes folk music. She likes Bob Dylan . . . there's a song by Bob Dylan on a tape someone made for her. She likes that. She played it this afternoon and she stood on the balcony.

Eric　What else?

Sylvia　She thought the fountain in the square looked nice.

Eric *gets up off the bed. He goes to the balcony. He looks at the fountain in the square. He comes back.*

Eric   Does she talk about me?

Sylvia   Sometimes.

Eric   Not always.

Sylvia   No.

Eric   But she talks to you. She asks you about yourself?

Sylvia   Yes.

Eric   You be careful, crow.
You're only here because of me.

Sylvia   I'm here because of her.

Eric   What exactly you want from her?

Sylvia   Nothing.

Eric   What exactly she give you?

Sylvia   Everything.

Eric   You watch your face, crow.
She belongs to me.

Sylvia   I belong to her.

Eric   OK.
OK.
We know where we stand.
I'm the boss.
Which is good. Good.
Because . . .
I might want you to do something for me.

Sylvia   Might you?

Eric   I might want you to find something for me.

Sylvia   You might prefer to employ a reliable man.

Eric   There might be no reliable man.

Sylvia   There never is.

Eric   This job might be too important. The thing might be too valuable.

Sylvia   What might it be?

Eric   A tape.
The man who has it is called Keith.
He's a Scottish civil servant.
I want you to find him, and get the tape from him.
I want you to bring it to me.

Sylvia   What's on the tape?

Eric   That's not your business.

Sylvia   How will I know I've got the right tape?

Eric   This man will know.

Sylvia   Why should he give it to me?

Eric   Steal it. If you can't steal it offer him any amount of money you can imagine. If he still doesn't give it to you, call me.

Sylvia   Sounds like it might be quite a job.

Eric   I'm sure you'll manage.

Sylvia   She'll miss me if I go away.
I look after her.

Eric   You'll come back.

Sylvia   I might not.

Eric   You will.

11

Bernard's *garden.*

Bernard *is sitting with his equipment.*
He is broadcasting snatches of music in different styles. The music registers on the computer in a graph of sound waves.
After each brief snatch an automated voice says.

Voice   Is this harmony?

After some moments, **Vivienne** *enters carrying a small heavy suitcase.*
A look between them.

Vivienne   Hello?

Bernard   I don't speak English.

Vivienne   I'm sorry?

Bernard   English. English? I don't speak it.

Vivienne   Oh. I'm terribly sorry.
I'm sorry.

Bernard   You're the woman then?

Vivienne   . . . ?

Bernard   The woman who's come to stay. The woman?

Vivienne   Yes.

Bernard   Here.

Vivienne   Yes.

Bernard   I'm Bernard.

He moves to shake her hand.

Vivienne   So am I.

Bernard   No. No. I'm Bernard. What's your name? What's
your name?

Vivienne   Vivienne. Vivienne.

Bernard   Vivienne.

Something of a pause.

Are you all right? Are you . . . you seem . . .

Vivienne   . . .

Bernard *moves to touch her. Draws back.*
She drops the suitcase.
She goes to pick it up.
He picks it up.

Bernard   Please. Let me . . .

Vivienne   I . . .

He touches her shoulder. Giving her strength for a moment.

Vivienne   I'm OK now really.

She is absolutely determined not to cry.

Really. It's just . . . I . . .
I'm embarrassed. I'm so sorry.
I . . . something quite unexpected and . . .
You're a stranger . . . please . . .
But . . . I'm OK. I'm OK.

Bernard   I understand.

Vivienne   I'm OK now.

Bernard   I understand, Vivienne.

Vivienne   It's OK.

Bernard   It's OK.

Vivienne   OK.

Bernard   OK.

12

The beautiful room in the fiat in central Oslo.

Night. The shutters to the balcony are shut.
The lighting in the room is low.
Nastasja *is sitting in bed, smoking. The bed is dishevelled.*
Eric *enters from the kitchen wearing a dressing-gown, carrying two
bottles of beer.*
He gives one to **Nastasja.** *She takes it.*

Eric   Why don't you switch on the radio?

Nastasja   OK.

She switches on a radio.

Static.
She tunes it. Finds nothing.

There isn't any music.

She switches it off again.
Something of a pause.

Eric Leave it on.

She switches it back on.
Static.

When I was a child, in Bergen, I used to listen to British radio
stations late at night. I sat at my window and watched the
lights of the trawlers as they moved out of the harbour into the
North Sea . . . and the signals from the station faded in and
out . . . shhhhshhhhshhhhshhhh . . . and the English bands.
I loved the English bands the DJs played. The ship's light
would move over the horizon. My pyjamas were made of
something . . . that thing pillows and sheets are made of . . .
that thing which is soft. I remember the first time I had
an orgasm my legs went numb and it felt . . . blue. I can still
remember that feeling exactly.
I love you. (*He touches her.*) I love you.
Take me in.
I wasn't a lonely child but I was lost at sea, that's for sure,
that's for sure and damn certain. Maybe I was sad. A sadness I
can never shake off I don't know. I don't know. You know I
went to a hippie festival in South Africa and there was not one
black face in the crowd. I danced with a white girl from
Johannesburg who was naked from the waist up, she had tiny
breasts and she'd painted her face with Hindu symbols. She
handed me a joint and it was the best dope, man, South
African dope is the best . . . the band played a Bob Dylan song
and she said . . . 'I love this song. Isn't this song amazing?'
And I said . . . 'Yeah . . . yeah . . . amazing.' And just for a
moment I thought . . . I actually understand what she means.
I'm with her. I'm here. And . . .
I want you.
All you.

Surrounded
Take me in.
. . .
. . .
Nastasja.

Nastasja　Yeah?

Eric　What are you thinking?

Nastasja　I'm thinking about my daddy.
He's up there.
He's watching over me now.
I really want to see him.

Eric　Is crow still out there?

He indicates the balcony.

Nastasja　Yeah.

Eric　Can she hear us?

Nastasja　Yeah.

Eric　I feel so sorry for Sylvia, you know.

Nastasja　She's had a hard life.

Eric　Yeah.

Nastasja　She has scars.

Eric　But what can you do? FUCK.
That's what it always comes back to.
Pain.
What can you fucking do about it?
Sometimes, I swear it seems so fucking pointless.
I mean you can do something. You do what you can.
You try to be civil but . . .
But I was at that hippie festival. A hippie festival.
And there wasn't a black face in the crowd.
They stood behind a fence.
And I'm there. My job. Is to . . . serve these people. Help
them to organise their lives. If they could only organise their

lives . . .
And for a moment you think you can communicate to them.
You smile. Don't you?
But then you realise.
What can you do?
Nothing.

Nastasja   Little Eric.
I wish I could make it better for you.

Eric   How can you possibly . . .

Nastasja   I can.
It's possible.

Eric   Where are you going?

Nastasja   I want to show Sylvia my daddy.

Eric   Sure.
OK.

Nastasja *goes over to the shutters and opens them.*
Sylvia *is standing outside on the balcony.*
Nastasja *goes out on to the balcony.*
Eric *lies back on the bed.*

Eric   Shhhhshhhhshhhhshhhhh.

13

On board Harmony 114.

The huge sound of a Soviet choir.
Oleg *is absolutely still.*
Looking towards **Casimir** *and earth, out of the window.*

14

In **Bernard**'s garden.

Nearly dark.

The computer is still broadcasting brief snatches of music.
The computerised voice asking.

Voice   *Is this harmony?*

Vivienne *has changed into summer clothes.*
She enters the garden.

The sound of wind in the trees.
She smells something. She looks amongst the plants and picks a handful of
leaves. She sniffs them.
She looks at the computer equipment.
She goes over to it and investigates it curiously, not touching anything.
Bernard *emerges.*
He is dressed smartly, wearing a suit but no tie.
Vivienne *hasn't noticed him.*

Bernard   This is my life. My work. My task.

Vivienne   Oh. I'm sorry.

Bernard   No. Please.

He shows her the equipment.

Every piece of recorded music the world's libraries can offer
me. Still no response. Come.

He leads her further into the garden. He points up at the moving satellite.

There it is.
Someone's up there watching us. Waiting for us to . . .
generate the right answer.
Of course, apart from myself we ignore it.
It sits there.
Like a teacher who comes into a roomful of noisy fighting
children and doesn't shout but stands quietly. A still point.
Drawing the kids attention one by one.
Until they're all ready to learn.

Vivienne   They're pretty.
It's pretty.

Bernard   Are you cold? You're not cold?

Vivienne   . . . ?

Bernard   I have food. I've made some food for us. Come.
Sit down.

*He leads her to a chair. She sits down. He goes inside. He comes out with
a bottle of wine and two glasses. He opens the bottle in front of her. He
makes a pretend struggle with the cork. She laughs. He pours out two
glasses. They sit and drink*

Vivienne   It's nice.

Bernard   . . . ?

Vivienne   It's good . . . ?

Bernard   Good. Good.

Vivienne   I was frightened about coming here.
But now I feel . . .
Is this mint . . . ?

She shows him the leaves she picked.

Bernard   Mint.

Vivienne   Mint.

Bernard   I don't know.

Vivienne   I don't know.

Bernard   . . . ?

Vivienne   . . . ?

They laugh a little bit. Relax.

Bernard   You're smiling. That's good.

Vivienne   The wind in the trees. Here I am in France.
Still alive.
Long live France!

Bernard   Long live France!

Vivienne   Long live France!

Bernard   You look happy.

Vivienne   On a mountainside. In a garden . . .

Bernard   Are you happy?

Vivienne   Just happy.

Bernard   OK?

Vivienne   OK.

Bernard   Good.

Vivienne   Good.

Quiet. The music and voice still going quietly.
Bernard *offers* **Vivienne** *a cigarette.*
She briefly refuses. Then takes it.
As **Bernard** *talks, he uses gesture strongly, at key moments, aware that*
Vivienne *won't really understand him but hoping, through a kind of*
cumulative effect, to get across his meaning. Even though she doesn't
understand, **Vivienne** *affects to out of politeness. Sometimes copying a*
gesture to indicate she has understood it.

Bernard   I shouldn't take one myself. I've had a stroke, you
know . . . my heart . . . It's a weak thing. I put too much strain
on it. Smoking. Drinking. Anger. All the traditional things.
The effort of . . . this. But still, it's my life, it's my work. I
refuse to be defeated. I don't have company up here. I'm on
my own. I've forgotten what it's like to talk to a person, let
alone a woman . . . so . . .
I used to work for the European Space Agency, you know,
maybe you haven't heard of it. We made rockets. I was
involved in a project to send men into space for a long period
of time, to see what would happen to them . . . to see if a
human mind . . . and body could stand . . . because if we are
to get to Mars or Jupiter never mind *Star Trek* . . . If we're
going to liberate ourselves from earth . . . we need to know the
human limitations.

Vivienne   *Star Trek.*

Bernard   *Star Trek.*
. . .
The Russians had a similar project. Probably the bastard

Americans, they colonise our minds you know.
Who knows?
We had all our early experiments on board the Arianne rocket.
You've heard of Arianne?

Vivienne   Arianne.

Bernard   In the jungle of the Congo we had established a launch pad. And all our equipment was there. Ready for the launch. It was so hot. A hot night in the Congo and Arianne looked beautiful . . . tall and white in the floodlights . . . I thought . . . look at what we're capable of. Look how extraordinary we are. The television crews were everywhere, the lights . . . how extraordinary we are.
. . .
And, of course, you know what happened. It was on TV of course. You know what happened? Yes?

Vivienne   Yes.

Bernard   . . .
She rose up slowly into the night . . . and then just as she began to arc towards the horizon . . . she exploded. She broke apart. Arianne consumed herself in front of us.
. . .
Which was my work of many years.
. . .
There was only silence.
. . .
I heard a physicist pray.
. . .
And then . . . for me . . . something also happened.
I also consumed myself.
My heart seemed to burst and I was surrounded by myself . . .
The lights and the heat seemed to pour into me . . . I think I fell on to the grass. My legs went numb. I heard a countdown in all the languages of the project . . . ten, nine, eight, seven, six, five, four, three, two, one . . . and I saw a girl, one of the assistants on the project running towards me . . . over the grass in the bright lights . . . . I tried to smile. I think she smiled back.

I don't know. That's the last thing I can picture . . . but I can
still remember the feeling absolutely precisely.
Blue. The colour blue.
So then hospital and learning to speak again and . . . of course
I couldn't work. So I have my pension and . . . I do this. This
is my work. This is my life. I've been on my own so long up
here I've forgotten what it's like to speak to someone. Let
alone a woman. I'm sorry. You're very polite to listen.

Vivienne   Bernard.
I hope you don't mind me asking this . . .
But . . .
Have you . . . the way you talk . . .
Have you had a stroke?

Bernard   So.

Vivienne   . . .

Bernard   OK?

Vivienne   OK.

Bernard   Good?

Vivienne   Very good.

15

The balcony of the flat in central Oslo.

Sylvia *and* **Nastasja**.

Nastasja   Such a little city. Tomorrow I'll take you to the
theatre. We won't understand any of the words but we can
watch the actors and . . . Ibsen used to sit in that café. I
learned the part of Hedda Gabler but they said I was too
young. Such a great man for such a small city. Isn't it good,
Sylvia? Isn't it amazing? Better than London. Better than that
tomb. There's a breeze. It's been so fucking shitty and hot all
day. I think maybe there's going to be a storm. He gave me
Ecstasy. I've got one more. I made him give me one for you.

Do you want it?

Sylvia *declines.*

Nastasja   I'm sure there's going to be a storm. A Viking storm. We can dress up and go like two ladies of leisure. And then when we stroll home across the square we can kick off our shoes and walk through the fountain. Isn't it good, Sylvia? Isn't it OK? The clouds are racing. Can you imagine. I think there's a storm coming. He's such a bastard but he's got the heart of child. I nearly had tears when he cried out 'cum baby cum for me cum baby cum'. Because there was nothing in me, Sylvia. Only this poor little boy. Look! Look! (*She points at the stars.*)
That's him. That's him!
That's daddy. I want him to see me.
I'm going up to the roof.

She turns towards the flat and finds that if she stands on the balcony rail she can reach a ledge. She begins to do this.

Sylvia   What are you doing?

Nastasja   I'm going up to the roof. I want to wave. I want to signal. Come on.

Sylvia   You shouldn't.

Nastasja   I'm not some fuck shitty English. Come on.

Sylvia   No. Nastasja . . .

Nastasja   It's easy.

Dangerously she pulls herself up to the ledge above.

Sylvia   I'm scared.

Nastasja   Why? Come up.

Sylvia *tries. She looks down. She stops.*

Sylvia   I can't.

By now **Nastasja** *is nearly on the roof*

Nastasja   You can see everything.

One can see everything.
There's a storm coming.

Sylvia   Where are you? I can't see you.

Nastasja   I'm at the top.
I can see him.
I'm waving at him.
I'm waving.

Sylvia   What's it like up there?

Nastasja   It's . . .
The clouds are racing.
Sylvia, you should come up.

Sylvia   What can you see?

Nastasja   I can see my daddy in the sky.
I can see the whole fucking shitty world.
You should come up.

Sylvia   I can't, Nastasja.

Nastasja   Get some music, Sylvia.
Get Bob Dylan.
Play that tape.
Look at all the people.
Aren't they funny in their little city.
Look at them.
I love them.

Sylvia *has gone inside. She quietly shuts the balcony doors.*

Nastasja   The fountain looks nice.
. . .
The fountain looks really really nice.
. . .
Sylvia, you can see all this . . .
All the . . .
. . .
You should come up, Sylvia.
Climb up.
It's easy and . . .

Sylvia, you can see all this . . .
Beautiful stuff.
All this fucking beautiful stuff.

16

On board the Harmony 114.

Oleg *recording the log.*

Oleg   This is the last entry in the log.
The mission is now over.
The results of the experiment are as follows.
The limit is this.
I am at it.
I can go no further through time alone.
I don't know what else to say.
If anyone finds this log . . .
I am over Europe. It is night. Moving east.
I have set explosive charges throughout the craft.
In a few moments the ship will consume itself.
Somewhere on earth is a woman I once loved.
Who has most probably forgotten me.
If she looks at the sky.
Or takes notice of the stars.
She may notice the disappearance of the Harmony module.
Or maybe not.
This is my final statement to her.
End of entry.

He switches off the log.
He removes the tape.
He puts on the first suit.
He puts on the helmet.

17

In **Bernard**'s *garden.*

Vivienne and **Bernard** *lying on the grass together.*
Bernard, *half sitting up, is caressing* **Vivienne**.

Vivienne　All I wanted was a clue. I'm sorry. A clue. Just a
. . . and the tie seemed . . . the picture seemed. But there isn't
anything. It's . . . I don't know if I can . . . I don't know if I can
do this . . . The message is meaningless. There's . . . A
mountain. Wind in the trees. I'm . . . maybe we shouldn't do
this . . . I'm . . . A garden. Grass. I don't want to be silly. I'm .
. . I'm not . . . I don't know what I'm doing. I've forgotten
what his face looks like. His face . . . I keep thinking of him
taking off his clothes. On the beach. Looking at the sea. And
was it raining that night? I don't remember. But I can't see his
face. I can only see . . . feel his shape. I'm not ready to accept
I'm . . . To feel . . . to feel this is . . . too much, too hard. Just
right now. Sorry. OK. Is that OK?

She sits up.

Bernard　OK.

Vivienne　Do you . . .

Bernard　I understand.

Vivienne　Good.

Bernard　Good.

Vivienne　I have to be alone . . . just for a moment. I'm
sorry . . .

She goes indoors.

Bernard *remains. He looks up at the stars.*

18

In space.

*We hear the computer continue playing snatches of music. We hear the
mantra, 'Is this harmony?'*

A sudden, silent, blinding flash of light.

19

The roof of the flat in central Oslo / In **Bernard**'s *garden.*

Bernard *and* **Nastasja** *looking up at the stars.*

Bernard/Nastasja   No! No! No!

Silence.
The sound of wind

Nastasja   DADDY!

Vivienne *runs into the garden.* **Bernard** *is lying on the grass. She approaches him. She lifts him up to a semi sitting position. He is alive. His body is limp. His facial muscles don't really work.*

Vivienne   Bernard? Bernard?
Are you OK?
. . .
OK?
. . .
OK.

Bernard   OK.

Vivienne   OK.

Bernard   OK.

Vivienne   What happened . . . ?

Bernard   (*A desperate attempt to speak which fails.*)

Vivienne   It's OK.

Bernard   (*A second failed attempt.*)

Vivienne   I know. I know. It's OK. I understand.

Bernard   . . . Good.

Vivienne   Yes.
Yes.

20

A bar in the West Highlands of Scotland.

A TV is on, broadcasting news. The sound is turned down.
The **Proprietor** *is reading a newspaper. He is facing the television but not looking at it.*

Keith *enters.*

Proprietor   Pint?

Keith   Please.

Proprietor *goes to pull pint.*

Proprietor   Don't speak Gaelic in here.

Keith   I'm sorry.
. . .
But you speak . . .

Proprietor   It's my language, you cunt.
You come here we talk it.
Mountains we can share.
Place names we can share.
But leave me my language.

Keith   I'm only learning.

Proprietor   Then stop.

Keith   Sorry.

Proprietor   You're the only one in tonight
Shite on the telly.
Fuck it.

Keith   I'll go if you want?

Proprietor   Fuck it. Stay. What's the difference?

Keith   Is it the news?

Proprietor   I'm looking at the paper. And there's a film I want to see. *One Crazy Motherfucker* it's called.

Keith   Sounds good.

Proprietor   It's set in an American high school.
There it's . . .
A cunt kills his dad in it.
He doesn't mean to like. But fuck it. It's a crime against
nature.
Don't try and tell me any different.

Keith   Why don't we watch it?

Proprietor   Reception's fucked. Always is on that channel.

Keith   What's on the news?

Proprietor   The policewoman that got murdered.
Folk are going fucking apeshit, man.
Flowers all over the fucking shop.
Folk can't take it anymore, I'm telling you.

Keith   It's terrible, though, it's . . . I was surprised how badly
it affected me.

Proprietor   She did not accept the situation.
I'm not saying she deserved what happened.
Nobody's saying that.
It's a tragedy.
But I'm saying you don't talk to people in that situation.
There are forces acting on a person's mind.
You have to understand the pressure.
The kid.
He's there. He's going crazy in the shop.
He's already making demands. You know, he's demanding.
He's shouting. He's saying.
'Give me what I want!'
And he's confronted by authority. In the shape of a
policewoman.
So there's your two forces. Woman, Authority.
His thinking is under pressure.
Rage. He's enraged.
His mind turns to a kind of lava. You know.
So she tries to negotiate with him.

But you don't negotiate with lava.
You run. You run away.
So she gets stabbed. She was not in tune with the situation.

Keith   She was pregnant. It's . . . too horrible to
contemplate.

Proprietor   She knows she's pregnant. She knows that. But
the kid doesn't know that. He has no understanding of that.

Keith   Why do you want to put her down?
She was brave, she . . .
She tried to talk to him . . .
What would you have done?

Proprietor   Lamped him.
I would have rolled up a newspaper.
We're in a newsagent . . .
I would have rolled a paper up.

He begins to demonstrate on **Keith**.

And stabbed towards his throat.
Umph.
He grabs his throat.
Knee in the bollocks.
And as he brings his hands down to protect himself his head
comes forward. Smash upwards into his eyes with two open
fingers.
RUN!
DO AS YOU'RE TOLD.
GET THE FUCK OUT OF HERE.

I'm on the radio.

With **Keith** *in the role of assailant. The* **Proprietor** *backs out of
the door to the bar, playing the role of policeman.*

Back-up.
I want back-up.
I'm leaving the shop.
Send all the fucking cars you've got down here.
I'm leaving the shop.

He shuts the door behind him.

Keith *is alone for a moment. With the television on.*
The television turns to static.
From his jacket pocket **Keith** *takes a mini tape recorder.*
He presses play.
The sound of breathing.
The door opens again.
Sylvia *enters.*
They look at each other.

Sylvia   Keith?

Keith   How did you find me?

Sylvia   I looked for you.

Keith   What do you want?

Sylvia   Only to talk.

Lights down.

Methuen Drama Contemporary Dramatists

include

John Arden (two volumes)
Arden & D'Arcy
Peter Barnes (three volumes)
Sebastian Barry
Dermot Bolger
Edward Bond (eight volumes)
Howard Brenton
  (two volumes)
Richard Cameron
Jim Cartwright
Caryl Churchill (two volumes)
Sarah Daniels (two volumes)
Nick Darke
David Edgar (three volumes)
David Eldridge
Ben Elton
Dario Fo (two volumes)
Michael Frayn (three volumes)
David Greig
John Godber (four volumes)
Paul Godfrey
John Guare
Lee Hall (two volumes)
Peter Handke
Jonathan Harvey
  (two volumes)
Declan Hughes
Terry Johnson (three volumes)
Sarah Kane
Barrie Keeffe
Bernard-Marie Koltès
  (two volumes)
Franz Xaver Kroetz
David Lan
Bryony Lavery
Deborah Levy
Doug Lucie

David Mamet (four volumes)
Martin McDonagh
Duncan McLean
Anthony Minghella
  (two volumes)
Tom Murphy (six volumes)
Phyllis Nagy
Anthony Neilsen (two volumes)
Philip Osment
Gary Owen
Louise Page
Stewart Parker (two volumes)
Joe Penhall (two volumes)
Stephen Poliakoff
  (three volumes)
David Rabe (two volumes)
Mark Ravenhill (two volumes)
Christina Reid
Philip Ridley
Willy Russell
Eric-Emmanuel Schmitt
Ntozake Shange
Sam Shepard (two volumes)
Wole Soyinka (two volumes)
Simon Stephens (two volumes)
Shelagh Stephenson
David Storey (three volumes)
Sue Townsend
Judy Upton
Michel Vinaver
  (two volumes)
Arnold Wesker (two volumes)
Michael Wilcox
Roy Williams (three volumes)
Snoo Wilson (two volumes)
David Wood (two volumes)
Victoria Wood

Title	Author	ISBN
Antigone	Jean Anouilh	9780413308603
The Hostage	Brendan Behan	9780413311900
A Man for All Seasons	Robert Bolt	9780413703804
Saved	Edward Bond	9780413313607
The Caucasian Chalk Circle	Bertolt Brecht	9780413308504
Fear and Misery in the Third Reich		9780413772664
The Good Person of Szechwan		9780413582409
Life of Galileo		9780413763808
The Messingkauf Dialogues		9780413388902
Mother Courage and Her Children		9780413412904
Mr Puntila and His Man Matti		9781408100707
The Resistible Rise of Arturo Ui		9781408111499
Rise and Fall of the City of Mahagonny		9780713686746
The Threepenny Opera		9780413390301
Road	Jim Cartwright	9780413623904
Two And Bed		9780413683304 (due 2009)
Serious Money	Caryl Churchill	9780413641908
Top Girls		9780413554802
Blithe Spirit	Noel Coward	9780413771971
Hay Fever		9780413540904
Present Laughter		9781408101483
Private Lives		9780413744906
The Vortex		9780413773098
A Taste of Honey	Shelagh Delaney	9780413316806
Accidental Death of an Anarchist	Dario Fo	9780413771575
Copenhagen	Michael Frayn	9780413724908 (due 2009)
A Raisin in the Sun	Lorraine Hansberry	9780413762405 (due 2009)
Beautiful Thing	Jonathan Harvey	9780413710307
Glengarry Glen Ross	David Mamet	9780413554208
Oleanna		9780413626202
Speed-the-Plow		9780413192806
Closer	Patrick Marber	9780413709509
Dealer's Choice		9780413714909 (due 2009)
Woza Albert	Percy Mtwa	9780413530004 (due 2009)
Entertaining Mr Sloane	Joe Orton	9780413413406
Loot		9780413451804
What the Butler Saw		9780413366801
Shopping and F***ing	Mark Ravenhill	9780413712400
Blood Brothers	Willy Russell	9780413767707 (due 2009)
Educating Rita		9780413767905 (due 2009)
Stags and Hens		9780413767806 (due 2009)
Crime Passionnel	Jean-Paul Sartre	9780413310101
Death and the King's Horseman	Wole Soyinka	9780413333605
Oh, What a Lovely War	Theatre Workshop	9780413302106
Spring Awakening	Frank Wedekind	9780413476203 (due 2009)
Our Country's Good	Timberlake Wertenbaker	9780413659002

Methuen Drama Modern Classics

Jean Anouilh *Antigone* • Brendan Behan *The Hostage* • Robert Bolt *A Man for All Seasons* • Edward Bond *Saved* • Bertolt Brecht *The Caucasian Chalk Circle* • *Fear and Misery in the Third Reich* • *The Good Person of Szechwan* • *Life of Galileo* • *The Messingkauf Dialogues* • *Mother Courage and Her Children* • *Mr Puntila and His Man Matti* • *The Resistible Rise of Arturo Ui* • *Rise and Fall of the City of Mahagonny* • *The Threepenny Opera* • Jim Cartwright *Road* • *Two & Bed* (due 2009) • Caryl Churchill *Serious Money* • *Top Girls* • Noël Coward *Blithe Spirit* • *Hay Fever* • *Present Laughter* • *Private Lives* • *The Vortex* • Shelagh Delaney *A Taste of Honey* • Dario Fo *Accidental Death of an Anarchist* • Michael Frayn *Copenhagen* (due 2009) • Lorraine Hansberry *A Raisin in the Sun* (due 2009) • Jonathan Harvey *Beautiful Thing* • David Mamet *Glengarry Glen Ross* • *Oleanna* • *Speed-the-Plow* • Patrick Marber *Closer* • *Dealer's Choice* (due 2009) • Percy Mtwa, Mbongeni Ngema, Barney Simon *Woza Albert!* (due 2009) • Joe Orton *Entertaining Mr Sloane* • *Loot* • *What the Butler Saw* • Mark Ravenhill *Shopping and F***ing* • Willy Russell • *Blood Brothers* (due 2009) • *Educating Rita* (due 2009) • *Stags and Hens* (due 2009) • Jean-Paul Sartre *Crime Passionnel* • Wole Soyinka • *Death and the King's Horseman* • Theatre Workshop *Oh, What a Lovely War* • Frank Wedekind • *Spring Awakening* (due 2009) • Timberlake Wertenbaker *Our Country's Good*

Methuen Drama Student Editions

Jean Anouilh *Antigone* • John Arden *Serjeant Musgrave's Dance*
Alan Ayckbourn *Confusions* • Aphra Behn *The Rover* • Edward Bond
Lear • *Saved* • Bertolt Brecht *The Caucasian Chalk Circle* • *Fear and
Misery in the Third Reich* • *The Good Person of Szechwan* • *Life of Galileo* •
Mother Courage and her Children• *The Resistible Rise of Arturo Ui* • *The
Threepenny Opera* • Anton Chekhov *The Cherry Orchard* • *The Seagull* •
Three Sisters • *Uncle Vanya* • Caryl Churchill *Serious Money* • *Top Girls*
• Shelagh Delaney *A Taste of Honey* • Euripides *Elektra* • *Medea*•
Dario Fo *Accidental Death of an Anarchist* • Michael Frayn *Copenhagen*
• John Galsworthy *Strife* • Nikolai Gogol *The Government Inspector* •
Robert Holman *Across Oka* • Henrik Ibsen *A Doll's House* • *Ghosts*•
Hedda Gabler • Charlotte Keatley *My Mother Said I Never Should* •
Bernard Kops *Dreams of Anne Frank* • Federico García Lorca *Blood
Wedding* • *Doña Rosita the Spinster* (bilingual edition) •*The House of
Bernarda Alba* • (bilingual edition) • *Yerma* (bilingual edition) • David
Mamet *Glengarry Glen Ross* • *Oleanna* • Patrick Marber *Closer* • John
Marston *Malcontent* • Martin McDonagh *The Lieutenant of Inishmore* •
Joe Orton *Loot* • Luigi Pirandello *Six Characters in Search of an Author*
• Mark Ravenhill *Shopping and F***ing* • Willy Russell *Blood Brothers*
• *Educating Rita* • Sophocles *Antigone* • *Oedipus the King* • Wole
Soyinka *Death and the King's Horseman* • Shelagh Stephenson *The
Memory of Water* • August Strindberg *Miss Julie* • J. M. Synge *The
Playboy of the Western World* • Theatre Workshop *Oh What a Lovely
War* Timberlake Wertenbaker *Our Country's Good* • Arnold Wesker
The Merchant • Oscar Wilde *The Importance of Being Earnest* •
Tennessee Williams *A Streetcar Named Desire* • *The Glass Menagerie*